Early Adolescence and the Search for Self

To our children Richard and Elizabeth

Early Adolescence and the Search for Self

A DEVELOPMENTAL PERSPECTIVE

Douglas Schave
&
Barbara Schave

PRAEGER

New York
Westport, Connecticut
London

Library of Congress Cataloging-in-Publication Data

Schave, Douglas.
    Early adolescence and the search for self : a developmental
perspective / Douglas Schave and Barbara Schave.
      p. cm.
    Bibliography: p.
    Includes index.
    ISBN 0–275–92765–2 (alk. paper)
    1. Adolescence. 2. Adolescent psychology—United States.
3. Self. I. Schave, Barbara. II. Title.
HQ796.S4116   1989
155.5—dc19   88–27514

Library of Congress Catalog Card Number: 88–27514
ISBN: 0–275–92765–2

First published in 1989

Praeger Publishers, One Madison Avenue, New York, NY 10010
An imprint of Greenwood Publishing Group, Inc.

Printed in the United States of America

The paper used in this book complies with the
Permanent Paper Standard issued by the National
Information Standards Organization (Z39.48–1984).

10 9 8 7 6 5 4 3 2 1

Contents

Foreword

Douglas and Barbara Schave have prepared a comprehensive review of early adolescence, which they characterize as a distinct and qualitatively different developmental phase. In cataloging the consequences of this stage, they call before us the work of Kohut, Krystal, Piaget, Offer, the Ornsteins, Basch, Marian Tolpin, Winnicott, Stern, Demos, and others. In so doing, the Schaves use their own experiences to integrate the work of these authors in a comprehensive presentation of early adolescence.

The early adolescent experiences a "softening" of his psychic structures; rapidly fluctuating and, at times, fragmented self-states result from the intensification of affect and the dramatic change in cognition. These disequilibria accentuate the adolescent's need for increased, but different, parental selfobject functions, while at the same time, this adolescent is to achieve self-integration.

Early adolescents use primitive defenses, such as disavowal, denial, projection, and regression to protect themselves from shame, and its variations—dishonor, ridicule, humiliation, mortification, chagrin, embarrassment, and disgust—as well as to stave off affect flooding. The early adolescent is egocentric; he has a special fable and an imaginary audience, more responsive than his unempathetic parents.

"Parents are often horrified by this new ever present emotionality and they often wonder when will this intensity calm down. They just want to bring some calm and sanity to their home life." Only when things calm down can the adolescent's psychic equilibrium return and these changes be integrated and consolidated.

The Schaves place the so-called "turmoil" of adolescence in this early phase. They view the quiescence traditionally viewed as late adolescence occurring during middle adolescence. Early adolescence is a period of great change, while adolescence proper is the occasion of self-integration.

They discuss, too, the nature of the psychotherapy of the early adolescent. Formal operations enable the adolescent to talk about new content in therapy, such as relationships with parents or life and death.

The Schaves hold that "sexual and aggressive drives, while significant, are only one aspect of a more central developmental process, that of narcissistic development or the development and the integration of the self facilitated by the affect attunement of parents and caregivers." It is the microinjuries of childhood that cause adolescents to need therapy. Their egocentrism, shame, disavowal, and denial cause them to resist psychotherapy.

The competent psychotherapist first fosters the therapeutic alliance by responding to the humanness of the early adolescent. "Silences are experienced as misattunements."

Regular contact with parents is essential to the treatment of the early adolescent. Therapy evolves into a new experience, with a new person, with a new ending, personality change, as the adolescent finds himself mirrored by the therapist.

When early adolescence subsides, everyone is better off and happier.

What we have here is an interesting journey into and through this most lively time of life. Their work once again emphasizes how adolescence is a unique developmental phase, not just a continuation of childhood, nor a simple reworking of childhood conflicts or traumata. Adolescence involves a complex transformation of the self in the context of its selfobjects. The psychoanalytic perspective is of how these transformations are experienced. To enter into the psychological world of the early adolescent is to embark on an intensely personal transition: a move toward increased competence, rather than autonomy; a thrust toward revised cognition, that many, but surely not all, adolescents achieve; an integration of sexuality and strong affect into the self experience, rather than being held as the province of the other. Parents do not cease to be important to the early, middle, or late adolescent; they simply are different. They continue to serve regulating functions, but in different fashions and modalities.

The Schaves recognize these differences and understand these modalities. Their discourse on early adolescence is a most valuable effort, an important component of the exciting contemporary endeavor to reformulate development and maturation.

Richard C. Marohn

Acknowledgments

We would like to thank those individuals who inspired us to write this book. Our fascination with early adolescence comes from both our personal experiences as parents and our professional experiences as psychotherapists.

We are grateful to our children, whose experiences contributed significantly to our understanding of the world of early adolescence. Additionally, by working together as parents of teenagers, we established new ways of interacting with our children, which were crucial in developing our conceptions about early adolescence.

Besides our experiences as parents, our professional experiences have been integral to the development of our perspective. We would like to express our appreciation to all of our patients for sharing their experiences with us and allowing us to reflect our ideas back to them.

Many people encouraged us to explain our ideas in the form of a written manuscript and we would like to thank them for believing in us. First, we would like to thank George Zimmar, Ph.D., senior editor at Praeger Publishers, for his personal and professional interest in this manuscript. George trusted our capacities to understand our children and our patients and to explain our insights to him; we hope that we have provided him with a theoretical framework that will be useful, both at home and at the office.

We would like to thank David Markel, M.D., for his help as an analyst, a friend, and a behind-the-scenes editor. His comments on a paper presented in 1985 in Scottsdale, Arizona, were instrumental in developing many of our main concepts. His comments at various stages of this book's development helped us organize the book and provided us with further material for our own introspection.

We would also like to thank John McNeil, Ed.D., professor of education at U.C.L.A., who not only encouraged us to write this book, but also read the manuscript from cover to cover at various stages of its development. Doctor McNeil's insights about content and organization of the text were crucial.

As the manuscript unfolded, many of our colleagues and friends read it and gave us valuable insights and feedback. These individuals inspired us to continue trying to explain what we wanted to say in a more understandable way. We are particularly grateful to Helen McDermott, M.D., Jona Perlmutter, M.D., Richard Rosenstein, M.D., Al Schrut, M.D., and Arnold Wilson, M.D., as well as Elizabeth Holtzman, Lena Pincus, Shirley Graham, Stephanie Ross, Kim Lefsetz and Elizabeth Karsner for their efforts on our behalf.

We would also like to express our gratitude to Richard and Judi Marohn for their friendship and encouragement over the years, and to Richard for his enthusiasm in writing the Foreword for this book.

We would also like to thank Judy Smith for her diligent efforts and assistance in the final preparation of the manuscript.

Introduction

Much like the early adolescents that we are writing about, this book describes a psychological and behavioral process that is continually evolving and changing. We will present a new viewpoint on the formation, development, and integration of psychic structure in early adolescents. Rather than viewing early adolescence as fraught with sexual and aggressive tensions, we view the struggles of early adolescence as part of a normative and healthy process of self-development. Rather than viewing young teenagers as only engulfed in a world of intrapsychic conflict, we regard them as active participants in an interactional process that begins at conception and contains the seeds of the struggles of early adolescence.

Four main themes are developed in this book: (1) the primacy of affects and affect attunement from infancy through early adolescence; (2) the continued importance of parents and caregivers in the development of the self; (3) the distinct affects or states of mind experienced by early adolescents; and (4) the phase of adolescence proper as a period of the consolidation of cognitive thinking and hence, of the psychic structure of adolescents.

We suggest that early adolescents' varying and oftentimes rapidly shifting states of mind are the result of their "quantum leap" in cognitive functioning. This entrance into formal operational thinking, which creates a psychological disequilibrium, is the genesis of the intensive vulnerabilities and egocentrism so characteristic of this age group. The vulnerability, the extreme egocentrism, and the ensuing arousal of shame are related to the increased need for external support systems to maintain psychic equilibrium. A lack of internal psychic equilibrium without external supports is experienced as a deficiency or "softening" of the ability of their psychic structure to maintain psychic equilibrium. The various hormonal, pubertal, and social changes, concurrent with the quantum leap in abstract thinking and the resulting egocentrism, result in the early adolescent phase being experienced as one of the most volatile times in their lives.

In adolescence proper, with the consolidation of their psychic structure, teenagers have a greater ability to take in, process, and relate to their world without the need for drastic internal changes or external supports; this facilitates a calmer time for older adolescents. The integration of the ego ideal, that psychoanalytic theorists view as the main task of adolescence proper, will be reformulated along a different developmental model.

We hope this book provides the reader with a unique viewpoint that will broaden and deepen their understanding of the mental, cognitive, and emotional development processes of early adolescence. In addition, we hope this book will stimulate further discussion on a very creative and often difficult time in life. We also recognize that we are, by the very process of making generalizations about this age group, doing an injustice to the strivings for self-integration of early adolescents in their "search for self."

ADDENDUM

On Mother's Day, 1988, Peter Boxenbaum, age 19, died of a myocardial infarction. His valiant fight with chronic renal failure since infancy was an inspiration to all who knew and loved him. Peter's life was an endless struggle. His courage to make his life meaningful to himself and those around him was remarkable.

Early Adolescence and the Search for Self

1

Characteristic Behaviors of Early Adolescents

SNAPSHOTS OF EARLY ADOLESCENCE

- A young female, dressed in punk clothing, walking with a teddy bear dangling under one arm.
- A talented and artistically gifted fourteen-year-old, who painted and sculptured for years with enthusiasm from everyone around her—parents, teachers, and friends—suddenly decides one day that she is a "terrible artist" and destroys all her works and never pursues this talent again.
- *The Diary of Anne Frank*, the touching diary of a fourteen-year-old who lived during one of the most horrendous time periods of the modern world. Anne Frank was able to articulate her own will to live and her sense of self in a profoundly meaningful way.
- Nervous seventh and eighth graders, desperately trying to fall asleep, their minds racing, thinking about starting a new school year the next day—Will anyone remember me? Will I look funny in my new clothes? Will anyone want to talk to me?
- The friendship of two boys in the movie *Stand By Me* shows how their friendship provides the strength to survive two destructive family environments. Their bond helps them leave the chaos of their small town in Oregon behind them.

How does one integrate these various snapshots of early adolescence into a coherent theory of psychological development? Our aim is to provide a different perspective on the phase of early adolescence by describing what we consider to be distinct characteristics of this age group. One of the unique characteristics of early adolescents is their dramatic shift or quantum leap in cognitive thinking from present to future orientation. This quantum leap in cognitive functioning provides the framework upon which all self-experiences are processed and integrated. As a result of these increased cognitive capacities, the early adolescent–parent dyad is reorganized and renegotiated as early adolescents begin a "search for self"—a self that is distinct and separate from the family. The intensity of cognitive and emotional disequilibriums during this phase leads to an egocentrism that activates very intense affects, such as shame, humiliation, and other related feeling states. Early adolescents protect themselves from these intense feelings, most particularly shame, by using primitive defense mechanisms, especially disavowal and denial. The extensive use of disavowal, and the resulting disconnection from the unconscious lives of these early adolescents, makes this phase developmentally unique.

EARLY ADOLESCENCE AS A DISTINCT DEVELOPMENTAL PHASE

We view early adolescence as a distinct developmental phase that is quantitatively different from both latency and adolescence proper. Early adolescence begins at about eleven years of age in girls and somewhat later for boys; it ends at about fourteen years of age in girls and somewhat later for boys. This phase is characterized by psychological changes that are developmentally unique in both the intensity and the reactivity of early adolescents to self-experiences and life situations. This intense reactivity, which leads to varying affect states, is often disruptive to the sense of self-cohesiveness as well as to the self-esteem of early adolescents.

Rapidly fluctuating, and at times fragmented, self-states are signs of the arrival of the phase of early adolescence. These highly volatile early adolescents can be intensely sad, angry, excited, and/or depressed within a short time span. Although these mood fluctuations are often seen as resulting from surprisingly minor situations or events, our intent is to develop a psychological framework based on observations that make the changing states of mind of early adolescents understandable.

First of all, many of the psychological vulnerabilities early adolescents experience are a function of a "softening" of their less intact psychic structures. This softening, or decreased ability to tolerate, assimilate, and accommodate changes, is precipitated by a dramatic cognitive disequilibrium—entrance into formal operational thinking. This cognitive change results in a psychic foundation that is intensely vulnerable to changes—even the slightest change in their external support system. This softening of the psychic structure creates difficulties in their ability to contain, modulate, and tolerate various affects and affect states. Furthermore, the growing cognitive capacity, coupled with the concomitant softening of their psychic structure, ironically often leaves these young teenagers with an acute sense of fragility and an impending fear of disintegration or self-fragmentation. This fear of self-fragmentation can even be sensed as the loss of their psychic foundation—even of their sense of self.

Second, the egocentrism of this phase is as equally distinctive and crucial as the cognitive and emotional disequilibriums as well as the psychological vulnerabilities these disequilibriums arouse. This intense egocentrism, caused by the quantum leap into formal operational thinking, fosters an intense fear of being exposed and shamed in front of parents, adults, and particularly peers. These disequilibriums also intensify the increased need of early adolescents for the selfobject functions their parents provided for them as younger children.

Parallel with this increased psychological vulnerability, are the struggles of early adolescents for increased independence and sense of psychological separateness from their parents. The manner and intensity of these struggles between early adolescents and their families have their genesis in the early adolescents' experiences as toddlers within the family constellation. In order to expand the boundaries of their world, young teenagers need to deny their parents continued importance. Yet, both toddlers and early adolescents, in spite of the intense states of ambivalence over these struggles, still need their parents to be available to listen to them, be emotionally available and responsive, set appropriate limits for them, and provide structure within the family to which they can turn when they feel disorganized or fragmented (Wilson, 1987).

In other words, early adolescents need their parents to continue to function as mirroring and idealizing selfobjects, in essence, to be there and to be affectively attuned to them. However, with conflicts over psychological separation/individuation and the ensuing ambivalence toward parents and independence, young adolescents experience a loss of psychological support from their families. The result is that an external source for the maintenance, repair, and further consolidation and integration of the self and psychic structure is unavailable at a time of greatest instability and need. The critical consequence of the perceived or real loss of family support, when coupled with the egocentrism brought on by the cognitive changes, once again forces an intensification of the shame and humiliation that early adolescents experience all too readily and frequently. Shame, the main disruptive affect of early adolescence, can be further differentiated into affects of dishonor, ridicule, humiliation, mortification, chagrin, embarrassment, or disgust (Krystal, 1982, 1982/83).

In summary, the softening of the psychic structure of early adolescents is manifested in feelings and reactions which include a sense of extreme vulnerability, a fear of exposure, and an overwhelming sense of mortifying shame. When these reactions of impulsiveness, moodiness, and extreme vulnerability are coupled with the perceived concomitant rejection of their parents as support systems or selfobjects, early adolescents experience a loss of being able to control and contain their affects. As a result, early adolescents tend to be highly egocentric, self-absorbed, and intensely ambivalent and fearful about their feelings. Their reactions to people and situations around them often cause others to perceive early adolescents as "the center of the universe" (Freud, Anna, 1936; Ornsteins, 1985; Schave, 1981, 1985). Simply stated, people involved with young teenagers simultaneously experience them as delightful, exciting, energetic, creative, and imaginative, and as supersensitive, moody, irritable, impulsive, demanding, and secretive. These typical early adolescent behaviors, at times compared to riding on a roller coaster by all those involved, leaves parents, junior high school teachers, or others who come in contact with them constantly trying to bring calm to situations that are all too frequently experienced as intense, disorganized, and fraught with struggle.

The flooding of affects, the heightened intensity of reactions, and the increased fear of being shamed or humiliated activate and perpetuate a specific set of primitive defense mechanisms. These defense mechanisms, which include disavowal, denial, projection, and regression, shape the way early adolescents perceive, assimilate, integrate, accommodate, and interact with their world.

The following chapters will help the reader understand the purpose and the meaning of various coping styles that early adolescents adopt and how their use alters the experiences, development, search, and ultimately integration of their sense of self.

"NORMAL" SOCIAL BEHAVIOR IN EARLY ADOLESCENCE

"Normal" social interactions for early adolescents differ quite dramatically from latency children or older adolescents. As school has tremendous importance in their lives, a description of early adolescence from a teacher's perspective will help illustrate how we view this age group. Martin, who taught high school before working with junior high school students, wrote about his experiences with early adolescents: "In the space of three years the change is drastic. At twelve (usually seventh grade) they are clearly on one side of limbo, at fourteen on the other" (Martin, 1971, p. 187). He viewed his high school students as people becoming adults; they looked like adults, had the size and shape of adults, as well as the physical and mental abilities of adults. He observed that older adolescents had clearly "become someone," while early adolescents were very different. Although they too were in the process of becoming adults, they were much more erratic, continually moving back and forth between the world of childhood and the world of adolescence.

In addition, Martin observed that although his early adolescent students made an instant and total commitment to a person, idea, or activity, their intense enthusiasm could just as quickly and easily be turned off or channeled elsewhere. His seventh and eighth grade students tended to be quite disorganized and many times had difficulty sorting out ideas. He observed that his students were often angry and discontented, but were unable to express their feelings verbally. Because of their inability to articulate their feelings, they frequently displayed physical anger, even females. However, when his seventh and eighth graders did express their feelings, the feelings seemed easily defused. In other words, just talking about what was going on inside themselves, in their inner life, was critical, even more so than the actual organization of these affective experiences. This can be easily observed and documented when one notes the amount of time early adolescents spend discussing a wide range of free-floating topics on the telephone.

Closely connected to requiring contact with others, and absolutely essential is membership in a group, which helps define the students' sense of self. Martin poignantly stated, ''There is a pain brought on by not being like everyone else when it is important that you be like others. This comes at a time in physical, emotional, and intellectual development when change is so rapid that many individual youngsters are either behind or ahead of the mass of their peers'' (Martin, 1971, p. 191). Martin likewise emphasized the extreme intolerance to diversity in this age group and how particular groups delighted in attacking and excluding those who were different.

However, while observing the desperateness of his early adolescent students to belong to a peer group, Martin also felt that they wanted and needed to be recognized for what they saw as special or unique about themselves. Conflict over conformity and individuality was a continual struggle for his students. Martin found that his capacity to affirm or legitimize their struggles over individuality was crucial in order for his students to feel better about themselves.

In summary, while appearing to thoroughly enjoy working with this age group, Martin experienced early adolescents as intense, erratic, brilliant, moody, and desperately seeking self-acceptance.

CHANGES IN COGNITIVE DEVELOPMENT: EARLY ADOLESCENCE

How does one explain the turmoil or psychological disequilibrium of this age group? The psychoanalytic literature has numerous summaries of adolescence (A. Freud, 1936, 1958, 1965; Erikson, 1950, 1959, 1968; Blos, 1967, 1970, 1979; Masterson, 1968, 1981; D. Miller, 1974; Rinsley, 1978, 1980; Berkowitz, 1983; Esman, 1985). There are also several studies from classical and self psychological perspectives (Marohn, 1977, 1979, 1981). However, early adolescence is rarely the primary focus of these studies. Even when early adolescence is addressed, the focus is on the eruption of the instinctual drives in which the ego is viewed as being overwhelmed by the id (GAP, 1968; Sarnoff, 1987), often resulting in a regression from oedipal strivings.

The authors feel that this viewpoint about sexuality, while important, does not fully explain the psychic life and struggles of early adolescence. To comprehend more fully the oftentimes erratic behavior of early adolescence, one must first understand the quantum shift in cognition that takes place from a Piagetian cognitive developmental viewpoint.

This shift, from concrete operational thinking to the beginning of formal operational thinking, is possibly the most drastic and dramatic change in cognition that occurs in anyone's life. This cognitive change contributes significantly to the disequilibriums—the confusion, chaos, volatility, and sensitivity—that early adolescents experience. The need for external supports that early adolescents require results in greater difficulties in processing and integrating their experiences on their own. In particular, they have difficulty integrating affects aroused by situations in which they feel out of control. Increased emotional struggles result as early adolescents experience a sense of tenuousness or softening of their psychic foundation.

Distinctions between the concrete operational thinking of latency children and the formal operational thinking of early adolescents are significant and crucial to our understanding of the importance and the impact of cognition in the psychic life of early adolescents. Piaget (1950, 1972, 1975) theorized that children and adolescents differ in their conception of what is real and what is possible. Concrete operational children tend to stick to the facts in front of them. Their hypotheses about their world are egocentric and concrete as they are based only on what is known or what is seen. Their hypotheses are also influenced by their animistic view of the world. They engender life to all objects, even inanimate objects around them.

Although concrete operational functioning latency children are far more logical than preoperational children, they are still unable to go beyond facts or the immediacy of their experiences. They know only what they see, hear, and experience. In contrast, early adolescents, upon entering formal operational thinking, begin with what might be possible and then decide what is reality. In other words, the less mature mind looks only to the factual relationship between one proposition and the empirical reality to which it refers; a more mature mind is able to look at the logical relationships between one proposition and another. This ability to think abstractly is the essence of formal operational thinking. Early adolescents who function at formal operational thinking are able to "follow the *form* of reasoning while ignoring its content, which is why the operations of this period are called *formal*" (Pulaski, 1971, p. 27, her italics).

While formal operational thinking usually begins around the age of eleven, this process does not reach equilibrium or stability until at least fourteen or fifteen years of age (ninth or even tenth grade). In some instances, research has shown that formal operational thinking is often attained later in life, or sometimes not at all (Flavell, 1977).

The quantum leap into a higher level of cognitive functioning makes life as exciting, confusing, intriguing, and frightening as the psychological world of the two-year-old. Like toddlers, who also experience a similar burst in cognitive thinking, early adolescents experience a dialectic of both the excitement of a rapidly expanding world, while at the same time experiencing the fear of becoming small or insignificant. This sense of insignificance, or a relative feeling of shrinking, is stimulated as massive amounts of information suddenly become available to be processed in a totally different way than before. Early adolescents are caught between "a rock and a hard place." They are still not able to totally leave the real world behind them nor are they free to totally enter the world of thoughts and ideas. However, this higher level of cognitive thinking changes the way in which young teenagers experience and integrate affect experiences—a crucial difference from the toddler a decade before.

Specifically, these new cognitive capacities allow for the development of an ability to build or understand ideas, abstract theories, or concepts without any regard to whether they have been previously experienced or actualized. This process allows early adolescents to become future-oriented. Dulit (1972) views this new ability as perhaps the most crucial development of formal operational thinking, for what counts in this stage is "what 'could be' and not merely what 'is' or 'was' " (Dulit, 1972, pp. 284).

Early Adolescent Egocentrism

Like all the previous cognitive changes, the quantum leap into formal operational thinking creates limitations for early adolescents. Specifically, these limitations include an extreme egocentric and self-centeredness in their behavior, appearance, thoughts, and feelings, as well as a perceived seriousness of their feelings. Young teenagers are unable to differentiate easily between what others are thinking about them and their own preoccupations. Almost invariably, early adolescents assume that other people are as obsessed with their behavior, appearance, thoughts, and feelings as they are. They assume that their subjective experiences are real and objective realities. These obsessions are the core of their egocentrism and create the following irrational components: the imaginary audience; the personal fable; cognitive conceit; the time warp (Schave, 1981, 1985), and assumptive reality (Elkind & Bowen, 1979; Elkind, 1981, 1984). As these irrational cognitive components are essential aspects of early adolescence, understanding them helps to explain many of the behaviors, appearances, thoughts, and feelings aroused in this age group.

The Imaginary Audience

"Stop looking at me!" "I know what you're thinking!" as they storm off in a huff. "I can't do that! I would rather die than have everyone see me with two different colored socks! How am I ever going to make it through the day?" or "I'll die if John (or Martha) sees me. I hate my hair!"

These examples illustrate the "imaginary audience," the belief of early adolescents that other people are as preoccupied with their behaviors, appearances, thoughts, and feelings, as they are—even when no one else is present. This belief results in a heightened self-awareness and an obsession about their behaviors and looks. Consequently, early adolescents often spend hours in front of the mirror worrying about their appearance—how they look to others. When early adolescents see a blemish or a spot, they experience an extreme sense of embarrassment or shame, as if they are being publicly displayed and ridiculed in front of an enormous audience. They are actually sensitive to anyone "looking"—they experience a hanging judge behind every look and smile. This sensitivity to people "looking" is particularly true when the "stare" comes from their parents.

Elkind (1981, 1984) defines this phenomenon as an "imaginary audience" because early adolescents truly believe that they are the focus of attention. The imaginary component is derived from the reality that in actual social situations, early adolescents are not the center of focus, at least not unless their actions cause everyone to notice them. Often, in trying to hide their "obvious defects," their attempts do result in their becoming the center of attention. This attention only confirms their deepest fears and suspicions—that everyone has been staring at them the entire time!

Elkind's conceptualization of the cognitive changes of this stage help us understand their increased self-consciousness, their fear of shame, and their resulting demand for privacy and secrecy. This cognitive change, which results in a sense of "Big Brother" watching, serves to exacerbate a deep sense of shame or fear of shame (Elkind, 1981). The belief in an imaginary audience is in part responsible for shame becoming the main affect during early adolescence and a major motivator for many of the behaviors and adaptations of this very sensitive and vulnerable age group. Further discussion of shame during the toddler period will be presented in Chapter Four; shame during early adolescence is described in Chapter Five.

Personal Fable

In reaction to being "grounded" for coming home late, young teenagers often state: "Mother/father, how can you do this to me? I can't believe it!—My own mother/father! Don't you know what this will do to me? I will never be able to go to school again!—You can't possibly understand that!"

This "personal fable" is a complementary function to the imaginary audience. With the personal fable, there is a development of an exaggerated sense of self-importance that makes early adolescents feel very special and unique. The personal fable is most evident in relationship to affect states. For early adolescents, this translates into a profound sense that only they can "suffer with such agonized intensity or experience with such exquisite rapture" (Elkind, 1981, pp. 91–92). From the viewpoints of early adolescents, parents cannot possibly understand how painful losing friends can be or how having to stay home because they came home late the night before will ruin their entire lives. This feeling is strikingly accurate in relationship to their belief that their parents cannot possibly understand their romances and crushes, particularly on movie or rock stars.

The intensity of early adolescents' feelings and thoughts affects other aspects of their lives because of the pervasive viewpoint of being the only person to ever think that, do that, feel that, or write that. Any adult, and parents in particular, who tries to share past experiences or feelings, are often looked at with disdain, disgust, or just plain disbelief. Early adolescents are prone to believe in the intensity and purity of their feelings and actions. This intensity and purity often causes early adolescents to experience life in black and white. There are no shades of grey. Adults who see differing shades of grey are criticized and condemned as unknowing, uncaring, insensitive, and inexperienced in spite of being grown-up.

Time Warp

"You can't do this!" "You can't prevent me from going to the movies with my friends! Hitting my brother/sister was yesterday! S/he started it! I told you I won't do it again! It's not fair!"

"Okay, from this moment on, I promise, I will never do that again! I swear I won't! I can't believe you won't believe me! There you go again! Always bringing up the past! You never give me a break! You don't love me!"

This "time warp" or the inability to link events or situations is another cognitive component that reflects the egocentrism of early adolescence (Schave, 1981; Schave, 1985). The time warp is the difficulty or even the inability of many early adolescents to form a continuum, that is, to allow events, situations, and especially feelings to be linked together. Early adolescents often do not allow a comprehensive sense of their own history to develop. They do not want to accept the fact that their behavior toward a sibling is resulting in their not being able to go out Saturday night. These same early adolescents do not want to accept the fact that poor grades on a test were due to their talking on the phone all evening instead of studying. Connecting these events could stimulate uncomfortable feelings such as guilt, remorse, shame, sadness or even anger; or the early adolescent, already in a vulnerable and chaotic state of mind, is fearful of the feelings becoming too much, too overwhelming. As a result, in many situations in which intense affects are involved, feelings are simply disavowed.

Because of the time warp, life events remain isolated and disconnected. The stronger the affects, the greater the tendency to disavow or dissociate feelings from these events or experiences. No wonder early adolescents, fearful of being overwhelmed by powerful affects and constantly struggling with increased self-consciousness related to the imaginary audience, often feel under assault from the outside world. The more intensely they experience being under assault, particularly with their lessened ability to organize and contain these experiences, the more early adolescents have to place responsibility for problems and issues away from themselves. The result is the compartmentalization and isolation of affects, events, or experiences through disavowal, massive denial, or projection. The use of these primitive defense mechanisms allows young teenagers to disconnect cause and effect from events, relationships, and any sense of linkage with time. The consequence is that early adolescents are free to start all over again—"That was yesterday! It doesn't matter anymore!"

While some degree of this time warp is evident in most early adolescents, its use becomes quite disruptive or pathological in early adolescents who experience severe self-esteem problems and have difficulty maintaining a psychic equilibrium. This description is especially accurate in relationship to families and school where troubled early adolescents are experienced by adults as uncaring, uncooperative, and defiant. With the massive use of disavowal, in particular, there is a breaking of the connection between events and affects. As a result, early adolescents no longer link their feelings, events, and thoughts together. This form of thinking also perpetuates the break with their past and their own unconsciousness encountered with latency children (Greenspan, 1979). For these early adolescents who need to deny feeling so out of control of their lives, any feelings experienced as too frightening continue to be split off and disavowed. In essense, patterns, or a personal history about their lives, are not allowed to be consciously formed.

Assumptive Reality/Cognitive Conceit

Another element of egocentrism is the intensification of the concept of "cognitive conceit." This conceit, which begins to emerge at the end of latency, is built upon "assumptive reality," the ability of early adolescents to detect flaws and errors in adults' reasoning and statements.

Two consequences result from this form of thinking. First, fed by the enormous influx of information suddenly available to them as they enter junior high school, young teenagers discover that they now can know more than their parents. Second, early adolescents often jump to the deduction that therefore adults are not very bright. Taking this line of logic even further, cognitive conceit grows into the assumption that if adults are wrong in one case of thinking, they must then be wrong in almost all other ways of thinking. Early adolescents then quickly assume that because they are right in one thing, they must be correct in most other things. Elkind (1981) suggests that this conceit is often fueled by early adolescents being unaware of the origin of their knowledge and believe that they come by it themselves.

Extremes of this conceited thinking are often fed by a low self-esteem and a need to be perfect or to be the "Mr. or Mrs. Know-It-All." These bright early adolescents, who need "to be right all of the time," have difficulties dealing with their parents and teachers in situations they find stressful or difficult. Instead, they use "This is stupid!" or "It doesn't really matter!" as a way to question classes they don't like or in which they are not doing well academically. Early adolescents with this attitude, particularly those who are having major academic and behavioral problems at school, cover up these problems by believing and stating: "It's not me! It's the class! It's the teacher!"

INTERACTIONS WITH PARENTS

Parenting early adolescents is an exciting time and parents particularly enjoy the dramatic changes in their children's emotional and physical growth, their creativity and imagination, and the expansion of their world. At the same time, being a parent of an early adolescent is also fraught with frustration, humiliation, futility, and rage. Parents, teachers, or therapists who work with this age group may be continually barraged with unbridled emotions that are disorganizing not only to the young teenagers' sense of self, but also to the adults' sense of competence and self-esteem. The intensity and abruptness of this phase has been described with accuracy and explicitness by parents during therapeutic consultations. Parents will often report that their calm and contained eleven-year-old is no longer as reasonable or reliable as s/he was just a few months before. Parents will say that their lovable child has turned into an emotional tyrant who slams doors whenever angry, who refuses to accept the rules of the household, and who seems so intensely ambivalent that it is truly frightening.

Parents are often horrified by this new ever-present emotionality and wonder when this intensity will calm down. They just want some calmness and sanity in their home life. Personal and professional experiences with these struggles of early adolescents have led us to reassure parents that this turbulent behavior will subside in time. Parents are advised that ninth grade and particularly the tenth grade are the pivotal years in the transition from early adolescence to adolescence proper. Parents, particularly when there are severe problems at home, are truly beside themselves and overwhelmed by the prospect of several more years of confusion and chaos in the lives of their children and, in turn, in their own lives. These tribulations cause their sense of competence as parents to be severely challenged.

Cognitive changes result in more than just volatility between early adolescents and their parents. The quantum leap in cognitive thinking and the new found social skills are essential for the more complicated theories and ideas presented in junior high school. However, early adolescents, already feeling more comfortable with their growing capacity to use combinational logic, can now look at a variety of alternatives which results in decision making becoming much more complex and confusing. Suddenly, young adolescents are loathe to accept the directives of their parents without question as they did only a short time ago. Early adolescents not only want to know *where* their parents stand, but also *why* they made a particular decision. Early adolescents are also instantly ready to defend their ideas or views over those of their parents and others with forceful and convincing logic. Elkind (1981) views quarrels early adolescents have with parental decisions as part of an indecisiveness about themselves and authority figures. Elkind also believes that this indecisiveness rather than automatically allowing for greater psychological separation from their parents, at times throws early adolescents into a new and even stronger dependence. As a consequence, Elkind believes that many times early adolescents seem to demand that their parents take a stand only so they can have something to rebel against, in order to feel more independent.

SECRETIVENESS/SOCIAL DISGUISE

One of the most visible, and at times, most frustrating behaviors for parents is their early adolescent's increased secretiveness about their thoughts and actions. Not only are early adolescents able to recognize that their own thoughts are private, but they now have the capacity to say things which are directly opposite to their feelings or thoughts. Younger concrete operational children and troubled early adolescents who have not yet entered formal operational thinking believe their fabrications and will defend them as the absolute truth. The healthier and more cognitively developed early adolescents know perfectly well what the truth is and yet, while not believing the fabrications, will defend their ideas and make them sound entirely convincing by backing themselves up with forceful logic. The results of this newfound capacity is an ability to use "social disguise." Social disguise is the ability to hide thoughts and wishes that may be quite different from the early adolescent's verbal assertions. More simply stated, early adolescents have the capacity to hide their true feelings and thoughts. While this can be used for social politeness, at the other extreme it can also be deceitful and can be used to exploit a situation.

DECREASED EGOCENTRISM: THE TRANSITION INTO ADOLESCENCE PROPER

We have provided an overview of the cognitive development that takes place prior to and during the phase of early adolescence. We have shown the impact of the quantum leap in cognitive functioning and its effect on the psychic lives of early adolescents. The resulting softening or fluidity of the psychic structure of early adolescents results in the emergence of an extreme egocentrism and the arousal of shame and related affects. We also discussed the use of disavowal to isolate or cut off these intense affects, which helps create the unique reactions of this age group.

Only as the vast changes—pubertal, hormonal, physical, and social— begin to calm down, can the psychic equilibrium early adolescents previously enjoyed return and allow them to once again rely more on internal supports. This firmer psychic foundation allows for the gradual integration and consolidation of these changes. With a firmer sense of self, early adolescents become even less externally oriented. This decreased need for external supports by early adolescents means that unsettling events or intense affects have less of a disruptive effect on their psychic structure, hence on their sense of self.

Only when their formal operational thinking and their psychic structure have consolidated, and the internal intensity of their affects have diminished can one say that early adolescents have entered adolescence proper. Adolescents are now able to maintain a higher level of cognitive thinking even in the midst of affect storms, states of confusion, or new situations. The ability to consider an increased number of possibilities, along with the ability to think about feelings abstractly, gives adolescents the opportunity to face and discuss such affect-laden issues as the relationship with their parents, problems with friends in school, sexuality, and even the meaning of life and death. All of these topics are intellectually far removed from the immediacy and overwhelming reality experienced only a few years before. Their system of thinking is now stable enough and flexible enough to tolerate great variations and intensities of feelings without necessitating internal changes (Greenspan, 1979). Cognition has now advanced to a level where the process of assimilation and accommodation, the dialectic of integrating their life experiences, brings in new information or adaptations to their environment without requiring massive fluctuations or confusion in their cognitive and emotional life. This is what Greenspan (1979) calls a "closed" or self-contained system. This system no longer requires the external help or external control needed by toddlers and early adolescents.

A LOOK AHEAD

Using the preceding outline of early adolescent thought and behavior as a framework, we will now discuss the integration of the affective life of early adolescents in order to give the reader a broad understanding of this distinct and crucial phase. To do this, our presentation follows a developmental sequence. Chapter 2 discusses the role of affects in the development and integration of the self. Chapter 3 delineates the role of parents and caregivers in the development and integration of the self or psychic structure, with a particular emphasis on the toddler phase. This chapter discusses the similarities and differences of parenting young children and early adolescents. Chapter 4 describes the integration of affect and cognitive development during infancy and childhood as part of the evolution of a set of organizing principles and the development of psychic structure. Chapter 5, building on these previous chapters, develops a perspective to explain the affective life of early adolescents. Included in this chapter is a description of how the individual's set of organizing principles and psychic structure of early adolescents becomes integrated. Chapter 6 reviews some psychotherapeutic techniques. Comments about the treatment of Narcissistic Personality Disorders, Narcissistic Behavior Disorders, and borderline psychopathology based on our theory of affect integration and cognitive development are presented. Chapter 7 briefly describes the transition from the phase of early adolescence into the phase of adolescence proper.

2

The Role of Affects in the Integration of Self

INTRODUCTORY COMMENTS

The Case of Dora

Sigmund Freud's "Dora—Fragment of an Analysis of a Case Study of Hysteria" (1905a) is the first reported case of the psychoanalytic treatment of an adolescent. Dora was an eighteen-year-old female who developed hysterical symptoms after her uncle attempted to seduce her. In spite of Freud's genius, he was unable to continue treating Dora for longer than four months.

Several factors seem to have precipitated Dora's termination from psychotherapy. One factor was Freud's apparent inability to understand Dora's emotional states of mind. Freud may have been distracted by his intense involvement with formulating his theory of infantile sexuality (1905b). Freud viewed Dora's repressed sexual impulses toward her father and her uncle as the main source of her emotional difficulties. He appeared unable to view her experiences of her uncle's seduction as an assault on her self, which then triggered feelings of shame, humiliation, disgust, and narcissistic rage. These questions remain unanswered. Did Freud fail to see or choose to ignore Dora's feelings about the seduction? Did Freud's view of females, which paralleled Victorian ideas about females, prevent him from understanding Dora's plight? Freud's treatment of Dora may have endured for a longer period if he had been able to accept and reflect back to Dora her feelings of shame, humiliation, helplessness, and anger.

A second factor in the treatment failure was Freud's countertrans-ference feelings toward Dora. Freud appeared to be too intensely in-volved in interpreting her dreams. Based on data from one of her dreams, Freud prophesized that Dora would flee psychotherapy. He became so engrossed with his own associations and ideas about her dream that he spent their last two sessions "informing" Dora what her dreams meant to her. It is quite probable that Dora's sense of being told how she thought and felt, as well as her feelings of being misunderstood by Freud through his interpretations, had much to do with her fleeing psychotherapy. Unfortunately, Freud's prophecy turned out to be ac-curate. However, when viewed from a self psychological perspective, the termination can be seen as caused less by Dora's acting out her repressed sexuality and more directly by Freud's misattunement to her affect states, particularly her feelings of shame (Lewis, 1987; Schneider, 1987).

While the above questions remain unanswered, many psychoana-lytically oriented adolescent psychotherapists continue to adhere to Freud's theoretical viewpoint and therapeutic stance. In doing so, these psychotherapists continue to focus primarily on issues of sexuality and aggression. They view these two primary instinctual drives and their integration as the main task of adolescence. From their perspective, this integration is essential in the process of the consolidation of the ego, or self. Because of this orientation, the major focus in the psychic life of early adolescents and interpretations in adolescent psychotherapy continues to revolve around sexual and aggressive issues.

Early Adolescence and the Search for Self illustrates how sexual and aggressive drives, while significant, are only one aspect of a more central developmental process, that of narcissistic development or the formation and integration of the self facilitated by the affect attunement of parents and caregivers. The development of healthy self-esteem and self-esteem regulation is also shown to be a crucial aspect of psychic development. The development of healthy self-esteem regulation is nurtured by ap-propriate affect attunement by parents and caregivers through their roles as selfobjects. These selfobject functions serve to provide the psycho-logical foundation and support that allows the child to handle most developmentally appropriate tasks without feeling overwhelmed.

Our perspective also focuses on the centrality of cognitive thinking in the development of self and the powerful impact changes in cognition have on how early adolescents relate to and integrate their self-experiences. In addition, early adolescents are viewed as active participants in an interactional process with their parents. This process, which begins in infancy, contains the seeds of the normative early adolescent struggles.

SELF PSYCHOLOGY: CONTRIBUTIONS TO UNDERSTANDING EARLY ADOLESCENCE

The writings of Kohut (1971, 1977, 1984, 1987) have revolutionized how many psychoanalytically oriented psychotherapists conceptualize psychic development throughout the life cycle. Greenberg and Mitchell state: "the basic constituent of Kohut's model of psychic apparatus is the self, 'a center of initiative and a recipient of impressions' " (Kohut, 1977, p. 99). . . . The self is no longer a representation, a product of the activity of the ego, but is itself the active agent; it therefore carries more theoretical weight than in the earlier views" (Greenberg and Mitchell, 1983, p. 353). Concurrently, infant researchers, such as Bower (1976), Ainsworth (1974), Demos (1982, 1983, 1984), and Stern (1985), have dramatically altered the perception of the infant–caregiver dyad by observing this relationship as being primarily interactional. At the present time, numerous psychoanalytic theorists and infant developmental psychologists agree that from birth, the infant has a distinct sense of self which is responded to uniquely by parents and caregivers. This book examines these newer concepts within the context of the formation, integration, and consolidation of psychic structure in early adolescents.

Self-experiences, affect attunement, and selfobjects are concepts that reflect a new way of thinking about the psychological development of infants and children. Parents and caregivers provide selfobject functions by performing essential psychological functions for their infants and children that they are incapable of performing themselves. While performing these functions, parents and caregivers are not experienced as separate individuals, but rather as part of their infant's or child's own self. These concepts can assist the reader in gaining a better comprehension of the varying and oftentimes perplexing states of mind of early adolescents.

Clearly, early adolescence is a frustrating and often misunderstood developmental phase for young teenagers and their parents alike. Psychoanalytical writers have tended to agree with Stanley Hall's (1904) conceptualization of this developmental phase as a time of *Sturm und Drang*—storm and thunder. Following Hall, A. Freud (1936, 1958, 1965) and Blos (1967, 1970, 1979) continued to view the turmoil of adolescence as being a direct result of the ego being overwhelmed under the onslaught of the rising hormones of puberty and the concomitant upsurgence of sexual and aggressive drives. In this theoretical perspective, the beleaguered egos of adolescents are seen as further threatened and weakened by the reemergence of oedipal conflicts. These oedipal conflicts result in the ego's regressing from genital sexuality to an earlier anal-sadistic state, fostering much of the self-centeredness and hostility of young adolescents. However, the authors believe that this theoretical orientation inadequately explains the core issues in early adolescence, including the "search for self."

Other theorists, such as Offer, Ostrov, and Howard, (1981) and Offer and Sabshin (1984) take the opposite point of view. They suggest that previous psychoanalytic theorists have overgeneralized the conflicts of disturbed adolescents seen in psychotherapy to that of normal adolescents. In particular, Offer, Ostrov, and Howard (1981) are opposed to postulating a theory of normal adolescence based on psychopathology. Their research, done mainly with older adolescents, suggests that adolescence is a relatively calm developmental period for the vast majority of teenagers. While the authors believe that Offer's theory may be accurate for older adolescents, we do not believe that this theoretical orientation adequately takes into account the intense developmental struggles of early adolescence.

Early Adolescence and the Search for Self provides a much more complex conceptualization of the dynamics of early adolescence and the struggles associated with this age group. First, the authors believe that adolescence can be separated into two distinct phases. The phase of early adolescence, approximately eleven to fourteen, is quite different cognitively, emotionally, socially, and psychodynamically from both latency and adolescence proper. These differences are due, in part, to the quantum leap in cognitive thinking, as described by Piaget (1950, 1972, 1975), which fosters a softening of the psychic structure of early adolescents. Young teenagers, because of specific changes in cognitive development, as well as hormonal, pubertal, social, and physical pressures that affect various aspects of their lives, become quite vulnerable to shifting and volatile states of mind and a sense of self-fragmentation.

As a result, they use defense mechanisms, such as disavowal, denial, projection, and repression. These upheavals cause early adolescents to be experienced by those around them as ultrasensitive, defensive, and temperamental. Often they are unable to accept responsibility for their struggles, difficulties, or insecurities. Their self-centered and irresponsible actions frequently lead others, particularly their parents, to experience them as "the center of the universe." Early adolescents act as if all life revolves around them—no one else matters. Ironically, at the same time, because of their search for independence, peers and adults outside of the family can experience the same youths as empathetic, caring, and dedicated.

In contrast to early adolescence, adolescence proper, approximately fifteen to eighteen is a phase where, due to the consolidation of the changes in cognitive thinking, an integration of self occurs. The consolidation of formal operational thinking, along with a relative calmness and a greater sense of stability, allows older adolescents to rely more on internal supports rather than on external supports. This greater sense of a firm foundation, the "solidifying" of the psychic structure of early adolescents, allows them to use more mature and sophisticated defense mechanisms, such as intellectualization, sublimation, and rationalization. As a result, older teenagers are more empathetic and involved with others, particularly with their family. This later phase finds adolescents feeling much more in control of their feelings, actions, and lives. They recognize their position as a satellite in orbit around a planet, as part of a larger unit—the family and society. With a greater capacity for this mutuality, older teenagers can view the world as being interconnected and having causality. They think about the possible consequences of their actions before they act. There is an awareness of a future. These older adolescents are very much like the adolescents described by Offer, Ostrov, and Howard (1981). They are ready to venture out into their world, whether as students, socially responsible citizens, workers, or partners in a mature relationship.

THE PARENTAL ROLE: RENEWED IMPORTANCE

Of utmost importance in the psychological development of early adolescents is the capacity of parents to help their children survive this intense and difficult but also very creative and rewarding phase of life.

The crucial nature of parental input and interaction with their infants, children, and early adolescents, is emphasized in our perspective.

Previous theoretical formulations viewed the development of infants from birth onward as governed by the internal forces of the instinctual drives. Any focus on parenting usually explored either the parental ability to fulfill basic physiological needs or more importantly, parental limitations in controlling and containing the primitive instincts of their infants and children. Our viewpoint, which we feel is much more inclusive, is rooted in recent theoretical formulations that view the infant–parent dyadic process as very active and central to the development of psychic structure.

Our perspective is based on two very critical and unique ideological developments that came to fruition in the 1970s. Both of these developments are basic to our developmental theory of early adolescence. First, infant researchers began to focus intensely on the innate qualities of the newborn infants. This focus allowed researchers to observe infants' and children's effects on their parents. The end result of this research is that child-rearing is now seen as a reciprocal process (Chess and Thomas, 1963; Ainsworth, 1974; Bower, 1976; Bell, 1977; and Demos, 1982, 1983, 1984; Stern, 1985; Demos & Kaplan, 1986). This viewpoint of child-rearing as "a two-way street" is discussed in detail by Stern (1985). Stern's view of the infant–parent dyad confirms what many parents have experienced with their newborn children—that infants and primary caregivers share an immediate and reciprocal bond.

Second, the critical contributions of Kohut (1971, 1972, 1977, 1984, 1987) distinguished two narcissistic transference phenomena, the Grandiose Self and the Idealized Parental Imago. Kohut postulated that these two narcissistic transferences reflect the two basic forms of nurturance infants and children require for psychological growth. Essential in his developmental perspective is the core concept of selfobject. Selfobjects perform psychological functions that parents and caregivers provide for their developing infants who are still unable to perform these psychological functions for themselves. Selfobjects are experienced as part of oneself and the "other" person is not considered or experienced as a separate entity. Parents and caregivers functioning as selfobjects are essential for the organization of the affective lives of their infants as well as the basis for the development of a sense of self or a set of organizing principles. Thus, Kohut viewed parents as the original archaic selfobjects, who foster the capacity of their infants to grow and develop. From this theoretical orientation, Kohut elevated the importance of parents and caregivers due to their providing two major self-object functions for their infants and children. The first function, mirroring, can be conceptualized as an emotional feedback system. Mirroring is the "gleam in the parent's eye" (Kohut, 1977), which infants instinctually see when they look up at a parent or caregiver after successfully completing a task. This gleam provides the beginning source of pride and hope in infants.

Kohut also recognized a second somewhat later function, idealization. Through the process of idealizing or looking up to parents and care-givers, infants experience parents and caregivers as all powerful, a "protective umbrella." This idealization also produces the beginning source of ambitions and goals.

In summary, when infants are seen as active participants in their own psychic development, then the conceptualization of an autistic state at birth and later a fused, symbiotic state influenced and controlled by instinctual drives, sexuality and aggression (Mahler, 1971, 1972), seems to have less of an impact on infant development than previously considered. Sexuality and aggression, originally viewed as the driver of human development, are not, however, discounted in our theory. Rather, they become secondary to the central role of affect integration and the development of narcissism and self-esteem regulation. Indeed, parents become valued facilitators (Demos, 1984; Demos and Kaplan, 1986) and integrators of affects and self-experiences, rather than valued only as controllers and regulators of primitive drive states or providers of the psychological needs of their infants and children.

The remainder of this chapter focuses on affect development of infants as viewed through the clinical contributions of self psychology and the more empirical contributions of the scientific methodology of infant developmental psychology. We will also define affect and its relationship to the search, formation, and development of self, or psychic structure.

THE ROLE OF AFFECTS IN THE SEARCH FOR SELF

The reason for the increased interest in affects and affect development is significant and profound. Affects can be seen as the basis of all relationships and the core of communication. In other words, individuals can best be understood by another individual through the communication of feelings, a process that begins at birth. In this way, affects become the organizers of self-experiences. Affects are the thread that remains constant throughout an individual's life. Simply stated, affects bring continuity to the human experience.

John Bowlby (1958) was one of the first psychoanalysts to write about the reciprocal interaction in the child-parent dyad. He described infants as having innate drives including sucking, clinging, and following. In these behaviors, infants are the initiators and principal active participants. In crying and smiling, two additional innate drives that Bowlby described, the infant's actions are seen as stimulating responsiveness. Mothers are the active participant only when their infants are crying or smiling (Bowlby, 1958). In our viewpoint, Bowlby's theoretical contributions become part of the foundation of modern affect theory because of his delineation of the reciprocal role between infants and parents.

Actually, the conceptualization of affect as a key motivator of interpersonal relationships and as central to human development originated with Darwin in 1872 (Demos, 1982, 1983, 1984). Darwin argued that particular affects humans display evolved primarily because of their value as preparatory acts and secondarily because of their communicative value. Darwin's emphasis on affects was overshadowed by Freud's revolutionary theory of infantile sexuality. While Freud's theory of infantile sexuality initially shocked the early twentieth century world, infantile sexuality became the accepted point of view among infant developmental psychoanalytic writers. Within this psychoanalytic framework, sexual and aggressive impulses are viewed as the primary motivators of the psychic development of infants and children. Unfortunately, within this theoretical perspective, affects came to be considered as only one minor element in Freud's theory of infant development, not a central focus, as in our perspective.

Serious opposition to the traditional psychoanalytic viewpoint was revived in the 1960s with Tomkins' research on the neurophysiology of affect. Nathanson, in an introduction to an article by Tomkins (1987), credits Tomkins rather than Darwin with developing the concept of the relationship of affect to facial display. For Nathanson,

Darwin saw the face as a passive and quite secondary vehicle for the display of emotion, which he believed to be a central experience appearing only later on the face. Tomkins recognized that the innate affects were manifested on the face with such rapidity, and were capable of such quick shifts, that they could not be explained as secondary phenomena (Tomkins, 1987, pp. 133–134).

Tomkins' research has paved the way for viewing affects as constituting the primary motivational system of personality (Demos, 1984). His theory indicates that an individual's affect system provides the primary blueprints for cognition, decision, and action. Tomkins believes affect states are regulated by both the individual's genetic endowment and by the way that s/he has been responded to and nurtured. In his theoretical formulations, Tomkins (1980, 1987), delineates nine primary affect states. The positive affect states, in their mild/intense forms, include: interest/excitement; enjoyment/joy; and surprise/startle. The negative affect states include: fear/terror; distress/anguish; anger/rage; shame/humiliation; and contempt and disgust. Within this theoretical perspective, affects become amplifiers of the human experience. Something good becomes better and something bad becomes worse. Another important result is that one can experience a rainbow of feeling states with various combinations and intensities of these affects. Tomkins feels that the regulation of these positive and negative affect states makes it possible for individuals to be free to control their own destiny.

Demos (1982, 1983, 1984) and Demos and Kaplan (1986), expanding upon Tomkins' theory, consider affects as primarily motivators of behavior. Affects are seen as distinct from physiological needs. Affects are also viewed as capable of being generalized to any situation. One can have a multitude of feelings about any event. From this vantage point, affects allow individuals the capacity and the freedom to dramatize or to elaborate upon events that are self-experiences. These self-experiences can be physical, cognitive, or instinctual.

This conceptualization of affects as the core or foundation of self-experiences is the beginning of a modern exploration of the role of affect and affect integration in the lives of newborn infants. Affects become essential to the development of self-cohesion and self-esteem regulation. They are developed through the interaction infants have with their parents and caregivers. In addition, Demos (1982, 1983, 1984) and Demos and Kaplan (1986) view affects as fostering the motivational thrust for interest, excitement, and enjoyment in life that will promote excitement and interaction with the world.

Basch (1977), also expanding on Tomkins' and Demos' theories, suggests that affect reactions are basic to the ordering functions of the brain. Basch differs with Freudian instinctual theory by suggesting that affects and cognitions are the basis of thought. Basch, following a Piagetian cognitive framework, believes that action promotes thought. This viewpoint runs counter to the traditional viewpoint that thought precedes action. Also, Basch, focusing on the importance of the infant-parent dyad, believes that parents and caregivers, through their affect attunement, serve as the quintessential selfobjects for newborn infants. Affect attunement allows for the sharing, confirming, and building of a sensorimotor model of cognitive thinking that is the basis of the infant's conscious and unconscious sense of self. Affect attunement also initiates the rudiments of the infant's set of organizing principles, in essence, the infant's early psychic structure. Equally important for Basch is the concept that only through affect attunement can the world of infants become a shared world—a world that is experienced as trustful and meaningful with significant others. Without this affect attunement from parents and caregivers, infants experience the world as solitary, private, and idiosyncratic (Tomkins, 1980). During infancy, one possible consequence of this lack of shared experiences is the creation of unconscious beliefs that the infant's affect needs are unacceptable and shameful.

Stern (1985) views infants as organizing their world around affect interactions. While Stern indicates that newborns relate realistically to their world based on their experiences, Stern does not suggest that newborns immediately experience a true sense of self. His observations indicate that there is a series of senses of self, beginning with an emerging sense of self. At birth, developing newborns are active in relating to the outside world and are capable of interacting with their parents and caregivers. Stern disagrees with Mahler (1971, 1972) by suggesting that newborns are psychologically separate from parents and caregivers and that they do not exist in an undifferentiated world that is either autistic at birth or later fused in a symbiotic state. Stern viewed the infant's first interactions as primitive and based on motor activity. These motor activities are similar to the sensorimotor schemas described by Piaget (1950) and Basch (1977). Stern (1985) suggests that infants have a feedback system based on a very simple sensorimotor system which is mature at birth and allows newborns to visually scan, discriminate, and inhibit eye contact with those around them.

Stern's observations are significant in terms of what we now realize infants are capable of processing both cognitively and emotionally. What appears to be of even greater importance is the focus Stern places on the interactive style or interpersonal world between newborn infants and their parents and caregivers. This interactive process plays a major role in meeting the needs of newborns and in setting the foundation and direction for the self-experiences of infants. For example, eye contact can be made and sustained by either infants *or* caregivers. More importantly, the needs of newborn infants can be respected by parents and caregivers by not forcing infants to sustain eye contact or to make eye contact when they want to be in a quiet state. Conversely, when the needs of infants are ignored by parents and caregivers, there is the potential for maladaptive interactions that can have enormous consequences for later psychic development. Thousands of these microexperiences between infants and their parents and caregivers begin to develop a history of expectations for infants.

Stern labels these expectations about the world as Representations of Interactions that have been Generalized (RIGs). For Stern, RIGs begin as episodes. Episodes are a combination of altering self-experiences of infants and the regulatory role of the other person that are not simply associated in a learned way.

Lived episodes immediately become the specific episodes for memory, and with repetition they become generalized episodes. . . . They are generalized episodes of interactive experience that are mentally represented—that is, representations of interactions that have been generalized, or RIGs (Stern, 1985, p. 110).

RIGs are prememory and preconscious and are generalized memories rather than a specific memory. However, they do approximate the development of a sense of expectations when confronted with new situations that have far-reaching implications for later life. RIGs are the foundation on which infants experience, relate, and organize the world around them.

New situations continually arise for infants that force them to organize new and unknown challenges. These periods are described as a dialectical process by Stechler and Kaplan (1980), paradoxes by Emde (1983), associational links by Demos (1984), moments by Pine (1985), and as episodes by Stern (1985). For Stechler and Kaplan (1980), the crucial issue is whether or not developing infants experience the challenge of new situations as being within their integrative capabilities. If the challenge is successfully integrated, there is then a new solution, positive affects are aroused, and the self is strengthened. When the challenge is beyond the infant's integrative capacities, they experience negative affects. As a result, attempts are made to ward off and defend against these negative experiences. This reaction results in a weakened sense of self. This dialectic exists from birth and continues throughout an individual's life. Infants, through countless self-experiences, gradually construct a self-structure consisting of these accrued affects and experiences of challenges that either add to their evolving psychic structure or weaken it. During infancy, parents and caregivers need to act as a protective shield, monitoring and regulating these self-experiences so that any incompatibilities are infrequent enough or they are not so overwhelming that they prevent infants from experiencing future new situations as manageable. In essence, parents and caregivers, through their capacity for affect attunement and their capacity to foster successful experiences, facilitate the laying down of positive RIGs, which allow infants to experience their world as exciting, even intense, but ultimately predictable and manageable.

SUMMARY

From our perspective what is important for the development of a cohesive sense of self which is able to function on its own behalf is the identification, arousal, toleration, and integration of affects, with the help of appropriate affect attunement from parents and caregivers. Affect attunement allows for the development of RIGs, a set of organizing principles, as well as the beginnings of a dynamic unconscious. As it is impossible in real situations to separate the integration of affect and the role of parents and caregivers in affect attunement, we now switch our emphasis from the arousal of affects in developing infants to the role of parents and caregivers as selfobjects.

3
Parents as Organizers of Self-Development in Childhood

THE IMPORTANCE OF THE INFANT–PARENT DYAD FOR PSYCHIC DEVELOPMENT

The emotional and intellectual capacity of parents and caregivers to foster and integrate self-experiences and associated affects of their infants has been underestimated in the classical psychoanalytic literature. Perhaps one reason for this oversight has been the primary focus on the developmental progression of the intrapsychic processes and the resulting internalized conflicts of infants. Beginning with Freud, psychoanalytic theories postulated that infants are born as amorphous masses, who slowly develop psychic structure as the result of the forces of instinctual drives, an internal process. The consolidation of this form of psychic structure culminates during the oedipal period with the emergence of a strong enough ego and superego which are able to withstand the instinctual pressures of the id.

This view has been encouraged for two reasons. First, theorists have tended to focus on the gratification of a child's needs as the primary element of the maternal role in the development of psychic structure. Second, theorists have tended to minimize the importance of the interactions between infants and their parents and caregivers, not just mothers. One consequence of this developmental viewpoint is the reinforcement of the conceptualization of infants as passive participants in their own psychological development.

Benedek (1959, 1970) was one of the first psychoanalytic writers to describe the role of motherhood within a psychosexual developmental

model. Within this model, a greater emphasis was placed on the interaction of the infant–mother when describing the psychological development of infants. Benedek (1970) suggests that maternal behavior can
be seen as emanating from two sources. One source is biological or
physiological. The second source is the mother's double identification
with her own mother as well as with herself as a child. The Ornsteins
(1985), commenting on this viewpoint, state that "although we agree
with Benedek in the essential aspects of her observations, we wish to
add that the biological roots of motherliness of the human female may
not only be 'modified,' but may actually be outweighed or totally overshadowed by psychological factors" (Ornsteins, 1985, p. 184). By
focusing on the psychological factors in parenting and the importance
of the interactions between infants and children with their parents and
caregivers, the Ornsteins strongly suggest that a "good enough" sense
of self as a parent is essential to the development and consolidation of
positive self-esteem as an adult.

Within the Ornsteins' framework, adults with a consolidated sense
of self will experience the task of parenting as an enrichment and
refinement of their sense of self. This enhancement of their self-esteem
is quite similar to the positive feelings provided by other creative and
artistic endeavors pursued as an adult. Likewise, adults with a poorly
consolidated sense of self will find the task of parenting highly disorganizing and fragmenting.

The Ornsteins, expanding on which factors help an adult to be a
"good enough" parent, suggest that empathy is crucial to understanding
parenting behavior. They view empathy as essential for the ongoing,
flexible maternal behavior that is necessary for a "good enough" infant–
mother dyad, or even better infant–parent dyad. From their perspective,
by focusing on the role of empathy, a mother's behavior can then be
viewed as part of a developmental line pertaining to the concept of the
self rather than Benedek's conceptualization of the process of double
identification, with a fixed and predictable pattern in parental responsiveness. By viewing the evaluation of parenting as integral to self-
development, the emphasis shifts from the "inevitability of repetition
and helps instead to conceptualize the way parenting itself provides an
opportunity for furthering the development of the adult self. This is in
keeping with Benedek's view that parenthood is a developmental phase
(Benedek, 1959) or rather, a developmental process (Brody, 1975),

which implies a structural rather than simply a behavioral change''
(Ornsteins, 1985, p. 201).

The Ornsteins' perspective, which highlights the narcissistic investment of parents in their children, suggests two critical factors related
to inadequate parental care. First, the failure of the selfobject ties or
narcissistic investment by parents in their children results in differing
types of abandonment. Infant abandonment can include the almost in-
comprehensible discarding of a newborn in a trash can, infanticide,
gross physical neglect, or equally as tragic, psychological abandonment.
From the parental side, the narcissistic nature of the child–parent ties
makes parenting such a vulnerable adult function and accounts for the
various forms of parental psychopathology, including forms of depression, anxiety, and guilt.

To help understand the process of parenting, the Ornsteins discuss
the concept of the "parenting unit." This unit can be comprised of
either or both parents or a group of persons who provide children with
the necessary responses for their psychological development. Being a
"mother" or a "father" no longer remains synonymous with parenting.
By introducing the notion of a parenting unit, the Ornsteins do not
intend to minimize the fundamental importance of the primary caregiver
in the development of attachment. "However, we wish to draw attention
to the infant's (and child's) capacity to elicit social responsiveness from
a variety of people and pets in the environment and thereby impercep-
tively compensate for the unavailable primary caretaker'' (Ornsteins,
1985, p. 184).

Closely related to the concept of the Ornsteins' parenting unit are
Muslin's view concerning mirroring and idealizing by parents. "Mirroring, per se, the human capacity to confirm and admire—whether it
involves support of verbal skills or admiration for the child's ability to
skip or jump—is not a function specific to any gender'' (Muslin, 1984,
p. 318). Muslin suggests that the issue is not the gender, but the ability
of parents to mirror their children. This capacity to mirror depends on
the stability of the parents' selfobject needs. A firm foundation allows
parents to empathize with their children's needs for admiration with
little tension, and/or rage, or sense of emptiness or loss. "The parent
who can allow her/himself to be the idealized parent—the target of the
child's need to put the mother or father on a pedestal to derive borrowed
strength in a potentially frightening world—is the parent who has had

appropriate idealizing selfobject relations in his/her life. These parents can empathize with the wishes of their progeny, can calm, soothe, lead, and allow the needed aggrandizing to take place'' (Muslin, 1984, p. 318).

THE CONTRIBUTIONS OF WINNICOTT: THE "GOOD ENOUGH" MOTHER

Freud suggested that the infant's skin functioned as a physical barrier or *Reizschutz* (Basch, 1975) to protect him/herself from too much input. Our perspective suggests that not only infants, but also parents and caregivers provide this stimulus barrier, or protective umbrella. Parents serve an extremely important function by modulating and filtering the emotional, cognitive, and physical stimulation levels to which infants are continually exposed.

The need for a stimulus barrier occurs at the moment of birth, when infants lose the all-inclusive protective environment of the womb. Newborns are immediately dependent on parents and caregivers because of their total inability to protect, regulate, or control any aspects of themselves or their environment. During the first several weeks, Winnicott (1953) suggests that parents or caregivers must function one hundred percent of the time to protect their newborns from overstimulation, hunger, cold, and the resulting pain and discomfort that these physiological states create. Winnicott's "good enough" mother is able to provide these regulatory functions and the protective barriers that newborns require. His concept of the "good enough" mother follows from the earlier works of Spitz (1945) and the Robertsons (1971), who observed infants' reactions to the loss of their primary caregivers. Winnicott's writings (1945, 1953, 1958, 1960, 1965, 1970) are crucial to our developmental perspective, as they help elucidate capacities of newborn infants for cognitive and emotional interactions. It is these interactions that lead to the formation and development of psychic structure. In other words, the concept of "good enough" mothering involves a very intense and active interaction between infants and their mothers and caregivers.

Cohler (1980) describes Winnicott as viewing the "good enough" mother as the director of the infant–parent relationship. The "good enough" mother's empathy is essential in the process of developing a sense of personal continuity. This process is similar in many ways to

Kohut's formulation of the role of empathy in the development of the self. However, unlike Kohut, Winnicott's perspective is based primarily on the object libidinal line of development. With this orientation, Winnicott's primary concern appears to remain with the development of satisfying relationships with others. As such, Winnicott does not appear to be particularly concerned with the formation of a capacity for the regulation of affect states associated with the development of the self. Summarizing, Cohler (1980) states that "for Winnicott (1945, 1951, 1960), as for Mahler and her associates, the mother is viewed as a need-fulfilling object rather than a source of soothing in the presence of tensions so intense that they can lead, if not regulated, to feelings of fragmentation of the child's fragile self" (Cohler, 1980, p. 92).

When looking at the important role mothers play in their children's emotional development, Winnicott and Mahler focus primarily on the abilities of mothers to satisfy basic bodily needs for their infants. Object relations theorists suggest that when "good enough" mothers are consistently able to meet their infants' needs, this type of regularity and constancy results in the capacity for loving and mature object relatedness to develop. This relatedness then fosters the capacity for internalization and the development of psychic structure. According to Cohler, Winnicott's orientation misses the importance of the affective development of infants in reaction to their maternal care. In other words, "Whereas Winnicott does speak of the 'good enough' mother who is empathetic with the child's needs (Winnicott, 1960, p. 591), he does not discuss in sufficient detail exactly what it is that makes the mother 'good enough,' or precisely why the mother's empathy is so significant for the child's development" (Cohler, 1980, p. 95). Additionally, Cohler views Winnicott's orientation of the "good enough" mother as implying a passivity in infants which is not in line with our perspective.

BEYOND THE "GOOD ENOUGH" MOTHER: PARENTS AS SELFOBJECTS

For an elaboration of the importance of being a "good enough" mother, Cohler (1980) turns to the writings of Kohut. Kohut's "good enough" mother requires more than just being dependable and consistent. For Kohut, what is essential is *the very soothing quality of her actions.*

Within this perspective, maternal care cannot be evaluated from an external frame of reference. Instead, as mothers make themselves available as selfobjects for their infants, we must understand how these interactions are perceived subjectively by children. Elaborating on this concept of the subjective experiences of children, Cohler states:

> Unlike Winnicott, Kohut recognizes that maternal comforting is not merely useful in promoting the infant's capacity for loving relatedness, but in facilitating the capacity for tension regulation associated with early grandiosity. The mother's ability to soothe her child by providing for successful regulation of tension is not just gradually internalized by the child from without, but begins by being perceived, originally, as residing within, as a part of the self (Cohler, 1980, p. 95).

When parents are enticed or encouraged to respond as selfobjects by the actions of their newborn infants, infants can then be perceived as a very active determinant of their own psychological development. This perspective provides for a clearer and broader understanding of what constitutes a "good enough" mother, or more importantly for us, a "good enough" parent.

Within this framework, Socarides and Stolorow (1984/85) and Stolorow (1987) conceive of the self as a psychological structure through which self-experiences acquire cohesion and continuity. They emphasize the importance and necessity of affect attunement between infants and their parents and caregivers. This integrative process consists of the accepting, affirming, differentiating, synthesizing, and ultimately integrating the various affect states of their developing infants. When these integrative processes are not provided by parents and caregivers, minute but significant derailments of optimal affect integration occur. When these various derailments are consistently present, affect states cannot be successfully integrated into the organization of self-experiences of infants. When this occurs, affects create self-states in which infants or children feel overwhelmed, and they become vulnerable to feelings of self-fragmentation. Consequently, when faced with a sense of self-fragmentation or disintegration, infants activate the defense mechanisms of disavowal, denial, and dissociation against these unacceptable and overwhelming affect states in an attempt to preserve the integrity of a constricted and fragile self-structure.

Within this selfobject framework, parents and caregivers provide several basic functions in the process of integrating affects and developing a set of organizing principles (Socarides & Stolorow, 1984/85;

Stolorow, 1987). First, parents and caregivers must be able to reliably recognize, distinguish, and respond appropriately to the distinct affect states of their children. Unfortunately, there are times when parents and caregivers cannot discriminate and respond appropriately to these affect states due to their own need to use their children as their selfobjects. When this reversal of selfobject functions occurs, infants or children experience severe derailments of their self-development. In particular, such situations seriously obstruct the process of self-boundary formation as the sense of self of infants and children cannot become clearly defined. In other words, if infants and children have to attend to the affect states of their parents because their parents are overwhelmed by a depression, anxiety, or preoccupation with other situational or internal stresses, then infants and children have no way of signaling to their parents disruptions in their own self-development. Optimally, infants learn to take care of themselves through the presence of their parents as selfobjects. When parents are unavailable, the developing sense of self of infants is left unattended and the infants' set of organizing principles or psychic structure does not develop in an adaptive manner.

The second function of parents and caregivers as selfobjects (Socarides and Stolorow, 1984/85; Stolorow, 1987) is their capacity to reliably accept, tolerate, comprehend, and eventually render intelligible the intense and often contradictory affect states of their infants and children as deriving from a unitary, continuous self. More simply stated, infants and children must experience their parents as being consistently accepting of all of their various affect states. There are times, however, when parents are psychologically unable to experience all affect states of their infants and children as emanating from a unitary, continuous self. In such cases, parents perceive their infants as "split" into two parts. There is the "perfect" child, whose "good" affects meet the selfobject needs of the parent and a second "alien" child, whose "bad" affects frustrate the selfobject needs of the parent. When this split occurs, the development of the affective synthesizing capacities and the corresponding advancement toward integrated selfhood of infants and children is severely obstructed. Consequently, the self-experiences of their infants and children become just as split off or fragmented as the internal states of mind of the parents. Rather than viewing this concept of splitting as a normal psychological process of a "good" and "bad" self and object representations during the toddler phase (Masterson, 1968; Kernberg, 1968, 1982; Mahler, 1971, 1972; and Mahler, Pine, and Bergman, 1975), the authors view this form of splitting as evidence of severe parental psychopathology. Such severe psychopathology results in multiple and consistent misattunements by parents and caregivers toward their infants and children (Tolpin, 1987). As shown by Demos (1982, 1983, 1984), Stern (1985) and Stolorow and Brandchaft (1988), when this type of infant-parent misattunement occurs, infants must move to where their parents are to preserve their tie. The result, as discussed in Chapter 4, is the development of a "false self," as suggested by Winnicott (1960).

The third function of parents and caregivers as selfobjects (Socarides and Stolorow, 1984/85; Stolorow, 1987) is to assist their infants and children in developing an ability to use affects as signals of disruptions to their internal state. The responsiveness of parents and caregivers and their ability to define varying affect states in their infants and children is what gradually makes possible the modulation, gradation, and containment of strong affects, whether positive or negative. When affects, regardless of their intensity, are perceived as signals of a changing self-state, rather than as indicators of impending psychological disorganization and self-fragmentation, infants and children are able to tolerate and accept their emotional reactions without trauma. They develop a sense that their world can handle disruptions, that life will be okay again, that things will get better.

However, without this self-signaling capacity and the appropriate response by parents and caregivers, affects are experienced as heralding impending traumatic states (Krystal, 1981, 1982, 1982/83). These intolerable affect states must then be disavowed, dissociated, repressed, or encapsulated through concrete behavioral enactments. For example, when parents are repeatedly unavailable to understand and acknowledge the loss and sense of self-fragmentation that their children experience from events, infants and children are unable to express the loss, the sense of fragmentation, and the resulting depression. Instead, these feelings of loneliness and depression may emerge in temper tantrums, aggressiveness with peers, encopresis, sleeping disorders, or a focus on sexualized thoughts or actions.

These potentially pathological, but self-protective efforts, literally cut off whole sectors of the affective life of infants and children from consciousness. In such cases, the emergence of affects often evokes painful experiences of shame and self-hatred in infants and children, which arise originally from the absence of positive, affirming responsiveness from their parents and caregivers. In these instances, emotionality becomes linked with a solitary and unacceptable state that must be eliminated at any psychological cost. Emotional trauma is viewed here not as an event or series of events overwhelming an ill-equipped psychic apparatus of a growing child. Rather, the tendency for affect experiences to create a disorganized, that is, traumatic self-state, is viewed as originating from early and faulty selfobject misattunements. This interactive process closely follows Stern's (1985) concepts of RIGs. While Stern clearly states that RIGs are not the same as selfobject functions, the RIGs formed by such repetitive negative interactions will form a very vulnerable or fragile self and negative set of organizing principles which results in a lack of psychic structure.

The fourth and final function of parents and caregivers as selfobjects (Socarides and Stolorow, 1984/85; Stolorow, 1987) is to foster the desomatization of affects. The repetitive verbal articulations of the initially inchoate, somatically experienced affects of their infants and children do more than just help " . . . the child to put his feelings into words; *more fundamentally, it gradually facilitates the integration of affective states into cognitive-affective schemata—psychological structures* [our emphasis] that, in turn, contribute significantly to the organization and consolidation of the self" (Socarides and Stolorow, 1984/85, pp. 110–11).

The role of parents and caregivers in the integration of the varying affect states of their infants and children can be best understood retrospectively through clinical material. An example would be a severely depressed parent or caregiver who is unable to tolerate the varying feeling states of his/her infant due to the caregiver's own lethargy and detachment from the world (Socarides and Stolorow, 1984/85; Stolorow, 1987). However, when parents and caregivers are able to tolerate, absorb, and contain the depressed affect states of their infants and children, they then function to "hold the situation" (Winnicott, 1965) so that these self-experiences can be integrated.

The responsiveness of parents and caregivers to the affect states of their infants and children is based on several assumptions. First, affect states, no matter how intense or long-lasting, do not threaten the organization of the sense of self of parents and caregivers. Second, parents and caregivers must also be available on a consistent basis to allow their selfobject functions to gradually become integrated in the form of a capacity for self-modulation of various affect states. This integration and capacity for self-modulation allows infants and children to assume a comforting and soothing attitude toward themselves. Consequently, intense and negative affect states will not entail irretrievable losses to the self, for either the parent, caregiver, infant, or child. When affect states are tolerated and accepted and when parents are "good enough" in serving these functions of their children, then the expectation that restitution will follow disruption becomes structuralized. A set of organizing principles is developed, which provides the basis for a sense of self-continuity and confidence for the future. These theoretical formulations closely approximate Stern's (1985) RIGs and Demos's (1982, 1983, 1984), and Demos' and Kaplan's (1986) detailed analysis of various forms of infant–parent interactions.

When parents are unable to tolerate feelings in their infants and children because various affects do not conform to the affect states, self-organization requirements, or selfobject needs of the parents and caregivers, they then are unable to help their infants and children in this critical task of affect integration. "When the child experiences such protracted derailments of affect attunement, he may, in order to safeguard the needed tie, blame his own depressive feelings for the selfobject failure, resulting in a pervasive, self-hating helplessness and hopelessness or—if he responds by defensively dissociating the 'offending' affects—in lifelong states of emptiness" (Socarides and Stolorow, 1984/85, p. 114).

THE PARENT'S ROLE IN THE FORMATION OF PSYCHIC STRUCTURE

More recent infant developmental research, including the works of Emde (1983), Papoušak and Papoušak (1983), Demos, (1984), and Demos and Kaplan (1986), also indicates the degree and intensity of the interactive processes occurring between infants and parents and caregivers. What these authors poignantly illustrate is the necessity for more than just the ability of parents and caregivers to provide the physical care and comfort to their developing infants and children or even to be "consistently available" to them. What these researchers deem essential for the formation and integration of a set of organizing principles or psychic structure is the affective interactions between infants and parents and caregivers.

Stern's (1985) recent infant developmental research is central to our conceptualization of the development and integration of psychic structure. Stern indicates that the ability of infants to sustain and/or break off interactions with parents and caregivers, as well as their need for appropriate responses from their parents and caregivers can be observed. At a very early age, newborns are able to fully use their visual-motor system to initiate, sustain, or even terminate visual contact with other persons. Stern's observational research strongly indicates the potential for misattunement when parents and caregivers do not respect the needs of their infants and children. These misattunements may occur when parents and caregivers force their newborns to continue sustained visual contact or when, because of a lack of attention by parents and caregivers, they are not available to initiate or maintain eye contact with their infants.

Stern's (1985) discussion of the "cliff experiment" is an excellent example of the infant–parent dyad on the development and integration of psychic structure. This experiment consisted of infants, their mothers, and a glass table with an illustrated "cliff" beneath the glass. The infants were allowed to crawl on top of the "cliff." When the infants reached the edge of the "cliff," they invariably looked to their mothers for a reaction. The results of the experiment are both predictable and fascinating. When mothers had a calm face and/or smiled to their infants, most infants continued crawling over the "cliff." When the mothers had an expression of fear or horror on their faces, the infants retreated from the "cliff," stopped exploring, and quickly moved away from this frightening experience.

Stern uses this "cliff experiment" to discuss the process and the effects of selective affect attunement. For Stern, affect attunement is the most potent way of shaping the subjective and interpersonal life of infants. Through this process of affect attunement, parents unconsciously transmit to their infants what is sharable and nonsharable. In other words, affect attunement becomes the *template* or mold for passing on desires, fears, prohibitions, and fantasies, all of which shape the psychic experiences of their developing infants. In these intense and complex interactions, which occur thousands of times every day, parents have to make a choice, usually out of awareness, about what to attune to or to focus on as infants provide almost every kind of affect state.

While successful affect attunement is essential for the healthy emotional growth of children, misattunements or "emotional thefts" are essential to understand, as they document the derailments and developmental arrests that occur between infants and parents and caregivers. For Stern, "successful" misattunements occur when a mother "enters" inside of her infant subjectively and sets up an illusion of sharing, while not actually sharing what her infant is experiencing. In other words, misattunement occurs when sharing is for the mother's emotional needs rather than for her infant's emotional needs. In this type of interactive process, infants are required to "move" to where their mothers "are" emotionally. Infants have to give up their own feelings and self-experiences for the needs of their mothers. To maintain this relationship, the needs or self-experiences of the infants must be disavowed or disowned. This maladaptive interactive process is forcefully highlighted in the very stimulating and provocative writings of Alice Miller (1981, 1983, 1984) who poignantly describes the tragic dilemma of gifted infants and children who are used by their parents for their own selfobject needs. Stern's concept of emotional theft is also reflected in Winnicott's conceptualization about the "true" self and "false" self (Winnicott, 1960). The "true" self has received appropriate mirroring. The "false" self is based on emotional theft.

Various interactions foster the experiencing of positive affects and either the encouragement or discouragement of their exploration. Demos (1984) lists six types of exchanges, out of many possibilities, each of which produces a distinctive positive or negative experience for children. Her view closely approximates Stern's (1985) RIGs in that "if such experiences become a chronic characteristic of the infant–mother system, then they will begin to shape the child's developing sense of self." (Demos, 1984, p. 19).

Demos and Kaplan (1986) illustrate the importance of parents and caregivers as facilitators during the first year of life by comparing the parenting patterns of two families with newborn girls. Donna's family maximized intense and prolonged affects. Challenges confronting Donna were generally kept at an optimal level that were within her expanding adaptive capabilities. On the rare occasion when the challenge went beyond her adaptive capabilities, the family responded with help and support which fostered a solution. Demos and Kaplan believe that optimally fostering growth and development in both positive and negative affects, as with Donna, produces an optimistic openness and expansiveness toward the world, and an experience of oneself as an active agent or participant toward the world. "By the end of the first year Donna is full of enthusiasm and zest and is the initiator of complex plans which she carries out with persistence and flexibility. She acts as if her wishes and feelings matter and conveys a general air of confidence that she can cause things to happen and can solve problems'' (Demos and Kaplan, 1986, p. 216).

In comparison, Cathy's family, her mother in particular, focused on shared interactions and kept Cathy's positive experiences brief and of moderate intensity. By keeping negative experiences to brief periods and at a very low intensity, Cathy's inability to tolerate these negative affects by the end of the first year began to interfere with her interactions with her world. Cathy's mother, by focusing on soothing and quieting activities, discouraged situations of experiencing herself as an active agent in her life. By her first birthday, while she enjoyed the social ambience around her, Cathy was often in a position of observer, rarely insisting on her social initiative. She had difficulties with strangers and received minimal assistance from her mother in learning to cope with these increasingly negative interactions. Because her mother protected her from intense positive and negative affect situations during her first year of life, Cathy often faced the world feeling overwhelmed as her current adaptive capabilities could not handle these increasingly uncomfortable experiences. As a result, the authors saw her respond with a constriction of her plans and initiatives.

Summarizing the family interactions and the effects on these two young females, Demos and Kaplan stated:

Donna's mother was able to tolerate Donna's expression of moderately intense negative affects and saw her role primarily as a *facilitator* (our italics) of Donna's efforts to cope with her own affects and their causes, intervening only when Donna was unable to manage the situation. This stance by the mother and the family in general allowed Donna to develop her affective competence by exercising and strengthening her capacities to modulate her negative affective states and to communicate her needs with affective signals. Cathy's mother did not allow her child to try in the early months and she saw her role primarily as a *nurser, soother, and comforter* (our italics). Thus Cathy was not given the opportunities to develop her own capacities for self-soothing, self-regulation, and modulation. By the end of the first year, Cathy is unable to fall asleep on her own, shows few resources for coping with moderately intense negative affect and has not developed the affective competence that would enable her to produce signal cries (Demos and Kaplan, 1986, p. 215).

The importance of the parent acting as a facilitator in the child-parent interaction, is also described by Demos (1984) in an example of a young child who suddenly grabs a pair of scissors in the presence of a parent. Demos described six interactive possibilities in this situation. Some mothers encourage continued curiosity and active exploration of the world, while removing the dangerous scissors from the reach of the child. Most examples show actions by the parent that discourage continued curiosity and active exploration. Later examples include outright stamping out of any curiosity while others include leaving the dangerous object in the child's world which makes the world a scary and unsafe place to play.

This child-parent interaction could just as easily be early adolescents and their parents, with early adolescents having problems at school, wanting to suddenly stay up later, go to a night club with a group of older friends, or wanting to stay out several hours later than usual to go to their first party. Parents who act as a facilitator for their early adolescents will encourage and foster active participation, including increasingly more decision-making responsibilities with the world. Parents will be available to facilitate increasingly more complex situations in which intense and sustained positive and negative affects can be experienced. When difficulties arise, whether problems at school, with friends, or even within the family, alternative ways of resolving the difficulties or impasse are explored and encouraged to provide and sustain a sense of continued competence. As a result, these early adolescents continue to see themselves as active and successful agents in their life, and they continue to maintain relative control of their affective life. Consequently, affects are experienced and used as signals for changing affect states rather than as a signal for fragmentation or self-disintegration.

SELFOBJECT FAILURES

Entitlement: Its Genesis

Whereas a lack of mirroring creates a depressed and selfless adolescent, other types of selfobject failures, which often have their genesis in the toddler stage, can create a complexity of misattunements that resurface in early adolescence. One misattunement occurs when parents fail to be facilitators of their children's self-experiences and treat their toddlers as psychological equals. In this "democratic relationship," parents relinquish their authority. These parents often experienced very painful childhoods themselves or recall their childhoods as idyllic.

There are two major underlying issues for this type of parenting. The first dynamic consists of parents who have not resolved psychic pain experienced during their own childhood and adolescence. These parents identify with the pain they assume their children will experience when they say "no" or "deprive" their children of something. These parents will do almost anything to protect their children from experiencing the perceived future pain. These parents state that they only "want their children to have the best." One consequence of this parental attitude is that parents have a difficult time setting limits or following through on consequences. As a result, there is an underdeveloped sense of cause and effect in their children. Bad manners, temper tantrums, screaming, no matter how upsetting to the parents, are always forgiven. The consequence of these parents' overidentification with the pain in their children and the parents' inability to say "no" results in the normal grandiosity, or a sense of self-importance, of the toddler stage becoming intensified.

An additional and essential factor completes the fostering of this archaic grandiosity and sense of entitlement (Tolpin, 1974; A. Ornstein, Gropper, and Bogner, 1983) that will haunt these families, particularly in early adolescence. This other factor is that these parents also feel, quite deeply, that they are not strong enough or important enough for anyone to listen to them, let alone do as they say. This can be seen in the market or at the park, whenever toddlers have a different idea of what they want to do than their parents. Trying never to say "no" and avoiding having to say "no," fosters a grandiosity and these toddlers begin to feel they can do what they want. Their parents will always let them have their way. When powerful affects arise, rather than having appropriate limits and having to learn to struggle and integrate these feelings, these children want to act in a way that avoids the frightening affects. They slowly develop a sense that they are "entitled" to do what they want. This sense of self-importance or entitlement usually returns in early adolescence.

This type of struggle is also hidden under the rubric of "family democracy." Within the concept of "family democracy" is the parental wish to have their developing children be equal members in the decision-making process of the family. Once these children enter early adolescence, the parents are confronted by young teenagers who not only expect, but insist on their rights. These entitlements can include having sexual encounters at their discretion with no intrusions by the parent, the expectation that they have the ability to go and come at their leisure, or the right to do what they want, when they want, if they want.

This sense of entitlement was evident in a family recently seen in consultation. This family of three, including a female early adolescent, appeared to be operating on what seemed to be a friendly and cooperative basis until their daughter reached junior high school. Suddenly, the family was engaged in battles with a young teenager who had never experienced disappointment, let alone feelings of being denied, and she was not willing to allow this painful process to start now. To experience disappointment or frustration was not acceptable. This was particularly true because underneath the facade of a very "together" young teenager was a very depressed, empty, and angry early adolescent who was terrified of experiencing the "black hole" that was the result of an earlier lack of appropriate parenting.

A LOOK TOWARD EARLY ADOLESCENCE

Just as the impact of parents and caregivers on developing infants is critical to the development of the self, the impact of parents on early adolescents is equally important. The same issues of affect attunement, mirroring, idealization, and the capacity to accept, tolerate, define, and integrate different affect states apply to young teenagers as well. For example, anxious parents will transmit feelings to their young teenagers in the same way the mothers in Stern's (1985) cliff experiment clearly indicated to their infants how they were reacting to the situation by the expressions on their faces.

What is different about infants and early adolescents is obvious. Infants lack the options, physically, emotionally, and cognitively, to be separate and independent. Therefore, they must depend unilaterally on parents and caregivers. Not so with young teenagers. Early adolescents can choose to rebel against the reactions of their parents and find selfobjects that are more attuned to what they feel they want or need. Early adolescents are capable, or at least feel that they are capable, physically, emotionally, and cognitively of carrying out this rebellion. Here lies the crucial issue for parents. How much structure and limit-setting do early adolescents require from the parents? The resolution to this issue is most likely "written" or laid out in the RIGs and later

FRIGs or *F*igurative RIGs of the interactions of the infant–parent dyad of years past. Parents who have been attuned affectively to their infants and children will have a better sense of the emotional needs of their early adolescents. These parents recognize the need to continue their selfobject functions, both in terms of mirroring and idealizing, as well as once again integrating affect experiences by accepting, tolerating, defining, and integrating the affect states of their early adolescents.

SUMMARY

Chapter 2 described how infants and children learn to interact and relate to their environment and how they develop a set of organizing principles. The powerful and essential role parents and caregivers play as selfobjects to their infants and children was described. It is through these interactions with parents and caregivers that their infants and children develop a sense of the world's dependability and reliability as safe or unsafe along the lines of Stern's RIGs. The importance of parents as facilitators rather than as directors throughout childhood into early adolescence was also described.

Chapter 4 will present a radical reformulation of the formation of psychic structure as it develops throughout childhood. Our viewpoint is framed within a developing Piagetian cognitive system. This cognitive viewpoint begins with sensorimotor thinking, proceeds through preoperational thinking, and ends with the concrete operational thinking of latency children.

4

Critical Developmental Issues in the Search for Self

WHAT IS PSYCHIC STRUCTURE?

The conceptualization of the development of psychic structure, or what we refer to as the process of developing psychic structure, is a crucial issue for psychoanalytic theorists. In Freud's original theoretical formulations, he postulated the topographical model (1905b) in which the mind was divided into two parts, the conscious and unconscious. Freud (1923), finding this model inadequate to explain fully his view of mental functioning, later postulated the tripartite structural model, composed of the ego, id, and superego.

Subsequently, psychoanalytic writers added the ego ideal as part of the superego, which is conceptualized as a set of values individuals attain as one of the major developmental tasks of mid- to late-adolescence (Anna Freud, 1965; Blos, 1967; Wolf, Gedo, and Terman, 1978). Overall, psychoanalytic writers believe that adolescence is a period to explore and define meaningful relationships to the family and society. Our book describes a perspective which allows for a different understanding of how these primary developmental tasks are initiated during early adolescence.

It is beyond the scope of this book to review the history of the development of psychic structure from a psychoanalytic point of view (Brenner, 1957, 1974, 1980; Hartmann, 1958) or from the viewpoint of many of its critics (Basch, 1976, 1977, 1982; Peterfreund, 1975a, 1975b, 1983; Schafer, 1968, 1979; Modell, 1981; Schwaber, 1983). However, a brief statement of the history and theory of the development of the self from a self psychology perspective is useful in understanding the process of the "search for self," which, in essence, is the process of the development and the integration of psychic structure during early adolescence.

PSYCHIC STRUCTURE AS A PROCESS

Over the last ten to fifteen years three major theoretical perspectives have been gaining momentum that have had enormous impact on understanding the development and integration of the self and its psychic structure. These three separate bodies of knowledge—the growing appreciation of the importance of a Piagetian perspective on cognitive development, new focuses on the activity of the infant–parent dyad in infant developmental research studies, and the emergence of self psychology as an all encompassing developmental theory—are creating major revisions in understanding what is essential for normal growth in infancy, childhood, and adolescence.

First, the seminal work of Piaget is vital to an understanding of the development and integration of the self. Piaget (1950, 1975) and his followers (Woodward, 1965; Pulaski, 1971; Dulit, 1972; Muuss, 1975; Flavell, 1977; Cowen, 1978; Elkind, 1981, 1984) have been able to elaborate on a system of cognitive development which helps explain the interactions between cognition, affect integration, and self-esteem regulation. The interaction of these elements creates a set of organizing principles or psychic structure that helps individuals understand and interact with their world in a unique and meaningful way.

Interestingly, many of the more recent theories of infant developmentalists, self psychologists, and classical psychoanalytic writers incorporate a Piagetian model of cognitive development into their theoretical framework (Basch, 1975, 1977; Greenspan, 1979; Stechler and Kaplan, 1980; Demos, 1982, 1983, 1984; Emde, 1983; Papoušek and Papoušek, 1983; and Stern, 1985). In a Piagetian model of cognitive development, individuals are in a continual state of dynamic equilibrium. The ability of individuals to understand their world is constantly changing through a process of adaptation. In this process a dynamic equilibrium is maintained through the continual interaction of assimilating new information and incorporating this new information by accommodating or altering the existing structure (Pulaski, 1971; Flavell, 1977; and Cowen, 1978). In other words, the world is adapted to by balancing what is perceived (assimilated) with the reality of what is experienced (accommodated). The very experience of integrating this new information into an individual's concept of the world modifies how s/he views and deals with his/her world. The process of assimilation and accommodation enhances or defines each stage, so that self-experiences are integrated in a totally individualistic manner at each level of cognitive functioning.

Basch (1977) summarizes how viewing the mental processes of infants and children from a Piagetian cognitive model enhances our understanding of the early stages of psychic development. In comparing Freudian and Piagetian mental life models, Basch suggests that both models are basically divided into two major components, unconscious or prethought and conscious or thought proper. For Freud, the basis of thought was the soma and the biological forces of instinct and drive. For Piaget, the basis of thought was the brain, that is, the sensorimotor schema function. Basch thus believes that Piaget's theory of cognitive development "eliminated the 'mysterious leap' between the soma and psyche which Freud found so puzzling. With Piaget's model it is possible to see how mental activity is an aspect of brain functioning and not the product of a new entity called 'mind' " (Basch, 1977, p. 256).

Our theoretical perspective follows Piaget's and Basch's theoretical orientations which distinguishes the process of cognitive development as separate and distinct from instinctual drives.

Infant developmental researchers, exemplified in the works of Demos (1982, 1983, 1984), Stern (1985), and Demos and Kaplan (1986), are at the forefront of a revolutionary way of viewing infants and the infant–parent dyad. Stern's and Demos's observations and discussions illustrate the high level of activity, the preprogrammed visual motor capabilities, and the crossmodal capacities of all senses of newborns. Most interestingly, these researchers both emphasize the separateness of the newborn and the intensity of the *two-way* interaction in the infant–parent dyad. This concept of infants as separate from their parents and caregivers is crucial to our conceptualization of the process of the development of psychic structure. Within this concept, infants are seen as immediately processing and reacting to stimulation based on their self-experiences, rather than from their instinctual drives.

The last component in our perspective on infant and child development includes the works of Kohut (1971, 1977, 1984, 1987) and the expansion of self psychology as a developmental psychology. Tolpin's

(1987) "cohesive baby," as well as the works of the Ornsteins (1980, 1985), Stechler and Kaplan (1980), Basch (1982, 1983), Socarides and Stolorow (1984/85), Stolorow (1987), and Beebe and Lachmann (1988) continue to focus on two factors: the cohesiveness and separateness of the newborn and young infant and the essential quality of the active dyadic relationship between infants and their parents and caregivers.

By integrating these three bodies of knowledge, we are better able to understand and explain the development and integration of psychic structure from infancy through early adolescence. In addition to integrating these three bodies of knowledge, we conceptualize the development of psychic structure as a process rather than as a "solid entity" built around the structural model of an ego, superego, and id. Throughout this book, the ongoing process of the formation, development, and integration of psychic structure is viewed as based on a very active and mutual interaction between infants and parents and caregivers. This active dyadic process continues throughout infancy, childhood, and adolescence. This mutual dyadic pattern sets a tone or pattern of interacting that creates a unique and distinctive psychic structure, or set of organizing principles for each individual.

Most basic to the development of a set of organizing principles or psychic structure is what Stern (1985) calls Representations of Interactions that have been Generalized (RIGs), or what Demos and Kaplan (1986) label associational linkages or affect sequences. RIGs are part of the development of self-esteem and self-esteem regulation. This process of developing a sense of a predictable and safe world becomes an essential component in the development and integration of self and hence, the development of a set of organizing principles, or psychic structure. With this in mind, we turn our attention to the formation of self-esteem.

SELF-ESTEEM REGULATION: ITS ROLE IN
PSYCHIC DEVELOPMENT

In a comprehensive review of the literature on self-esteem and self-esteem regulation, Cotton (1985) bridges the various disciplines of psychoanalysis, psychiatry, social psychology, child development, education, and sociology. Using a developmental model, Cotton states that "the developmental line of self-esteem should highlight the progression from simple, more isolated structures and functions to more complex, integrated regulatory processes for the maintenance of self-esteem'' (Cotton, 1985, p. 123). Cotton's concept of the development of self-esteem regulation is quite similar to our concept of the formation and development of a set of organizing principles, or psychic structure.

Paralleling Greenspan's (1979) cognitive model of the process of change, Cotton (1985) reviews six principles that characterize the development of self-esteem regulation. First, during times when the formation of the self is undergoing change, there is a sensitive or vulnerable period for the formation of positive self-esteem. This sensitive period occurs at all developmental levels, with each developmental level building on the previous ones. Second, during periods of ''new learning,'' such as during shifts or quantum leaps in cognitive thinking, there is a return to the need for external sources to support self-esteem. Third, one's self-esteem is conversely lowered as an individual moves from one developmental level to another as these quantum leaps often result in massive turbulence and confusion. Fourth, one's self-esteem is enhanced as each developmental level is successfully negotiated and an increased sense of competence or effectance, that is, control of one's world, is consolidated. Fifth, during the course of development as individuals consolidate their cognitive shifts, they move from relying exclusively on external sources of self-esteem to greater dependence on internal sources for support. This greater reliance on internal support allows for a greater sense of being in control. Sixth, self-esteem will always depend to some extent on the recognition, validation, and praise from external sources, even when life is under a dynamic equilibrium. The turbulence and resulting reliance on external sources for support and at times its unpredictability during movement between developmental levels is what we believe contributes to the ''softening'' or ''fluidity'' of psychic structure. Likewise, the consolidation of a developmental level and the return to more internalized support and hence, a more balanced system, is what we describe as the ''solidifying'' or ''hardening'' of psychic structure.

Cotton's review of the literature concerning self-esteem and self-esteem regulation focuses on three major functions that appear necessary for the development of positive self-esteem and smooth self-esteem regulation.

The first function is the effects of the esteem of others on developing children. Through the esteem of others, information about what is worthwhile and lovable about oneself develops. This idea closely parallels

Stern's (1985) theoretical view of how the hopes, fears, and fantasies of parents and caregivers form a template in the transmission and development of positive and negative traits to their children. This concept also parallels Demos' (1982, 1983, 1984) and Demos' and Kaplan' (1986) clinical descriptions.

The second important function is the development of a sense of competence, that is, the sense of being successful. Competence develops out of a basic experience of effectance, with effectance defined as "the motivation to act on the environment to gain a predictable consequence" (Cotton, 1985, p. 124). When infants learn that they can cause something to move, change, or disappear in some way, they develop an increased sense of competence. This increased sense of competence then leads to an increased sense of mastery over their environment. Continued experiences of gaining mastery over their environment results in infants developing a sense of increased positive self-esteem. However, when infants learn that they cannot cause something to happen, there is an increased sense of frustration, or lack of a sense of mastery over their environment. This lack of mastery leads to a sense of a lack of competence and effectance. Continued experiences of not gaining mastery over their environment results in infants developing a sense of decreased or negative self-esteem.

The last function is the self, which is viewed as a selective filter of the first two functions (Cotton, 1985). Although initially separate, these functions become increasingly intertwined as development proceeds. The self establishes a sense of regulation through the process of organizing and integrating the multiple sources of self-esteem, such as the selection of information, the assignment of value to different sources, and the synthesis of contradictory information from these sources. This process of repeatedly organizing and integrating the multiple sources of self-esteem becomes one of the important components in the development of a set of organizing principles or psychic structure for infants.

AFFECT INTEGRATION: ITS ROLE IN PSYCHIC DEVELOPMENT

There are a number of infant researchers and theorists whose views on the importance of processing and integrating information for the development of a set of organizing principles or psychic structure parallel Cotton's. Demos (1982, 1983, 1984) and Demos and Kaplan (1986) describe the self as a gradually evolving psychological structure that possesses organizational and integrative properties. They suggest that what is most crucial to the development of an organizing structure is the integration of affective and cognitive components of self. They suggest that affect plays an extremely important role in the development of self and self-esteem regulation. Affects are viewed as providing the motivational thrust, excitement, and enjoyment which promotes the interests and curiosities of infants to explore their world.

These researchers stress that infants must learn through the presence and support of their parents and caregivers to manage and regulate the intrusion of negative affects into moments of "I" experiences, when infants can observe, explore, and interact with their world by themselves. The ability to tolerate these negative affects is derived from past experiences of parents and caregivers successfully modulating these affects for their infants. This modulating by parents and caregivers allows infants to sense that their affects do not routinely escalate out of control.

They also note that since infants have to be able to experience and sustain their positive affects, parents and caregivers must not only sustain these feelings of interest and enjoyment for themselves, but also share them with their infants. When this occurs regularly, infants develop an increased capacity to sustain positive feelings about their self-experiences and to allow and tolerate affects associated with these self-experiences. It is through this gradual expansion of infants' interests that the basic components of positive self-esteem are laid down.

Our viewpoint encompasses the theoretical formulations of Stechler and Kaplan (1980), who view the adaptive processes of infants successfully negotiating or completing affect tasks as fostering the development of self-regulatory functions. Each successful mastery of an affect task results in a higher order or new level of organization being developed. These more integrated and complex sets of organizing principles and more developed psychic structure are, in turn, then available for creation of newer and even more complex solutions, hence, even higher sets of complex organizing principles of the psychic structure. Stechler and Kaplan (1980) believe that the evolution of these self-regulating functions into a set of organizing principles is what was previously described as psychic structure. Additionally, these authors are not comfortable with terminology, which over the years has come to imply the possible translation of a psychic process into a solid entity, such as the psychic structure of ego, id, or supergo. Instead, these authors, like ourselves, conceptualize the psychological consequences of integrating experiences of infants as the development of an increasingly complex set of organizing principles that facilitate self-regulation, that is, psychic structure.

REPRESENTATIONS OF INTERACTIONS THAT HAVE BEEN GENERALIZED: RIGS

Stern's (1985) conceptualization of Representations of Interactions that have been Generalized, RIGs, allows for a major reformulation of the concept of the development of psychic structure in infancy and childhood. These major reformulations are increasingly important for conceptualizing what occurs in early adolescence, which is the next period when such extensive changes in one's set of organizing principles or psychic structure takes place.

Stern's RIGs are preconscious, prememory, and preverbal. With the new capacity for preoperational thinking, the toddler phase allows for the "laying down" or development of a new set of RIGs. The RIGs of toddlers are at a higher cognitive level in that they are "attached" to symbolic or figurative thinking. These *F*igurative *R*epresentations of *I*nteractions that have been *G*eneralized, or *FRIG*s continue to be formed and shaped by several factors, including the cognitive level of children as well as the interactive processes of the child–parent dyad (Demos, 1982, 1983, 1984; Stern, 1985). It is at this time, with the addition of symbol formation, that the dynamic unconscious, which is seen as the basis of psychoanalytic developmental theory, evolves (Basch, 1977; Stolorow and Atwood, 1987; Stolorow and Brandchaft, 1988). Like RIGs, these FRIGs are formed on the basis of the quality, intensity, and quantity of the interactions between toddlers and their parents and caregivers.

From our theoretical perspective, we do not believe that there is a "normal" process of splitting. With "good enough" parenting, RIGs and later FRIGs are laid down which provide a sense of the world that is dependable and consistent. In other words, children develop a sense from interactions with their parents and caregivers that life experiences, including disruptions to the self, will eventually work out. Our concept of "good enough" also implies that when parents and caregivers make mistakes or errors, they are capable of recognizing and acknowledging these errors and that they are "good enough" to correct their misperceptions and misattunements. Winnicott's (1960) concept of mutuality in the infant–parent dyad lays the foundation for affect attunement (Socarides and Stolorow, 1984/85; R. Stolorow, 1987). Affect attunement views the distinguishing, recognizing, tolerating, and accepting of the various affect states of developing infants and children as crucial to their psychological development and the development of a set of organizing principles, or psychic structure.

For Demos and Kaplan (1986) and Beebe and Lachmann (1988), psychic structures are developed or acquired when "a set of organizing principles become represented as the predictable 'rules' of the relationship" (Beebe and Lackmann, 1988, p. 20). These rules are based on two separate processes that function in parallel. First, there is the recognition of the crucial role positive affects play in the development of psychic structure. Positive affects cannot be taken for granted. Rather, positive affects must be actively accepted and encouraged by the parents. This is by no means a passive process. In order to develop a strong enough sense of the importance of these feelings, such as joy and excitement, parents and caregivers must also be able to experience and enjoy these positive feelings comfortably themselves, while sharing them with their children.

Second, they also suggest that psychic structure develops through children having to deal with negative affects. This process appears to be somewhat analogous to Kohut's optimal frustration and transmuting internalization (Kohut, 1971, 1977, 1984, 1987). In this process of internalization, there are countless times during a day, even during a single interaction between children and parents and caregivers, when children do not experience their parents as providing a "good enough" amount of their selfobject needs. When parents cannot provide their selfobject functioning at a rate that is developmentally appropriate for their children, then their children experience micromisattunements. Hopefully, the children experience these misattunements at a level of optimal frustration not overwhelming by being too intense, too long, or too frequent. This sense of the misattunement being "just enough," or within the developmental capabilities of infants and children, allows them to start to take in or to internalize part of the selfobject functions of their parents, that is, transmuting internalizations. This process of transmuting internalizations is what Kohut (1971, 1977, 1984, 1987), Tolpin (1978, 1980, 1983, 1987), and A. Ornstein (1981, 1983) define as the process or formation of psychic structure.

Bacal (1985) and Stolorow and Brandchaft (1988) question the concept of optimal frustration, particularly in relationship to their work with adult patients. Rather than accepting the concept of optimal frustration, they both propose a concept of optimal gratification. For these authors, optimal gratification represents the therapist being available, as optimally as possible, to provide the selfobject functions required by their patients. This concept has important implications for infant development as well as the formation and development of a set of organizing principles, or psychic structure. Whether using optimal frustration, optimal gratification, or optimal responsiveness (Bacal, 1985) during infant development, Demos and Kaplan (1986) state that there are separate lines of development for positive and negative affects. Within these two development lines, at different times, the concepts of optimal gratification or optimal frustration may be relevant in helping to understand the formation of a set of organizing principles or the building of psychic structure. The concept of parents and caregivers being *optimally responsive*, whether through optimal frustration or optimal gratification, to supply the appropriate selfobject needs to their children becomes crucial in the development and integration of their set of organizing principles or the building of psychic structure from infancy through early adolescence.

PSYCHIC CONFLICT: ITS ROLE IN PSYCHIC DEVELOPMENT

The concept of psychic conflict becomes relevant to self psychology theory when the interactions between infants and parents and caregivers are examined. Stolorow and Brandchaft (1988) are instrumental in illustrating how infants learn that they need to "change" or "move" to where their parents and caregivers consciously and unconsciously want their infants and children to be in order to maintain the selfobject ties. This need, often unconscious, sets up psychic conflict in infants and children as they must give up a part of their self, their own needs, or their desires to continue to provide selfobject functions for their parents. This interactional pattern forms the RIGs and later FRIGs, which are part of the set of organizing principles or psychic structure of the infants and children. Stolorow and Brandchaft (1988) suggest that the needs of children to "change" or "move" sets up a pattern of self-in-conflict which focuses around two overlapping processes.

One area of psychic conflict centers around the consolidation of a nuclear sense of coherence, well-being, self-confidence, and ambitions. Here, the basic needs of infants and children are for appropriate mirroring responses and for their connection to idealized sources who provide a sense of comfort and strength. Affect states connected with this developmental process include pride, expansiveness, efficacy, and pleasure in oneself. Other affect states include willful rebelliousness, emergent sexuality, and competitive aggression. "When such mirroring responsiveness is consistently absent, because the child's developmental strivings and accompanying affect states are injurious to the parent's sense of well-being, then such strivings and feeling states become the source of severe and enduring inner conflict and guilt" (Stolorow and Brandchaft, 1988, p. 247).

The second area of psychic conflict centers around the differentiation of the self from others. Here, the needs of infants and children are for the continuation of selfobject ties that can serve as a source for affirming, facilitating, and solidifying support in their strivings for self-delineation and the establishment of individual goals and values. Sources of structuralized conflict in this area include affect states that are reactive to threats or injuries to the self and/or ruptures in the bond with their selfobjects. A sense of oneness and an idealized source of strength and calm provided by the parents and caregivers with their ability to reconnect or repair their children's ruptures assist in the integration of such disruptive affect states as anxiety, sadness, disappointment, shame, guilt, and rage. When such attuned responsiveness is consistently absent, due to the reactive affect states of infants and children threatening the self-organization of their parents, infants and children experience a loss of their parents and caregivers. With this loss, the painful feelings of infants and children remain unintegrated and become the source of wrenching inner conflict, self-hatred, and a lifelong vulnerability to traumatic states.

THE TODDLER: PREOPERATIONAL THINKING

The Development of Symbol Formation

The process of psychic conflict becomes "fixed" during the toddler period with the consolidation of the cognitive transition from sensorimotor thinking into preoperational thinking. This cognitive foundation provides the "solid ground" which toddlers use in their strivings for independence, autonomy, and self-assertion. Prior to this consolidation, however, when the cognitive foundation is fluid and more vulnerable to external pressures, there is a heightened egocentrism. This heightened vulnerability, along with the increased reliance on external support systems, results in an increased propensity toward the activation of shame. Because we view shame as a primary affect during this phase as well as the core affect in early adolescence, we will next review the concept of shame.

SHAME: ITS EFFECT ON PSYCHIC DEVELOPMENT

Shame has been associated most closely with toilet training in infant development. Erikson (1950, 1959, 1968) highlighted the struggle for early mastery and the battle of the wills for toddlers who were unable to compete physically or psychologically with parents. Throughout his works, Erikson, maintaining a psychosexual developmental viewpoint, suggested that this conflict was part of the anal phase, part of the anal-sadistic struggles with parents. However, it is our belief that individuation, at any age, whether expressed through separation or mastery, is always vulnerable to shame and a sense of impotence, and is not necessarily related only to an anal-sadistic state.

Lovitz (1985) summarizes that, "A review of the psychoanalytic literature on the subject of shame from Freud (1905) to Wurmser (1981) places most discussion and understanding of the shame dynamic within the structural or topographical model . . . In that model, shame is viewed as an affect arising from instincts, drives, and unconscious conflicts between the id and superego or between the ego and ego ideal" (Lovitz, 1985, p. 5). Lovitz discusses Morrison's (1984) viewpoint of shame as the core of a narcissistic patient's pathology. While agreeing that shame reflects feelings of defect and failure, "it does so in the context of an affective relationship. Shame is an affect testifying to the fact of a disruption of an affective bond" (Lovitz, 1985, p. 6).

Feelings of shame and impotence are quite powerful and often over-whelming. When one feels ashamed, one *feels as though* there is no way to relieve the problem and there simply is no way to restore the balance of things. According to Kaufman, "*one has simply failed as a human being*" (our emphasis) (Kaufman, 1985, p. 8). These feelings are so painful and so degrading, that experiencing shame activates a series of other feelings. First, a fear of further exposure to shame is activated. This fear, in turn, stimulates an instant flash of self-protective rage. This self-protective rage, whether expressed outwardly or internally, protects children against further exposure, but paradoxically prevents them from either healing the inner wound or reuniting with the person who caused the shame. Unfortunately, the end result is that there is no repair of the ruptured tie, and hence, there is no escape from the inner loneliness of these children. When shame is experienced too frequently, the vital sense of basic trust with parents and caregivers is betrayed, if not destroyed.

Kaufman (1985) described how easily the child–parent dyad can become caught up in a vicious spiral of shame and rage when toddlers are striving for autonomy and independence. Kaufman repeatedly emphasized the importance of parents acknowledging to their children their previous inability to recognize or meet their children's needs. In other words, parents need to acknowledge their own limitations and take responsibility for the child–parent interaction. By doing so, parents relieve the terrible burden of their children feeling that it is all their own fault. Through the acknowledgment of their responsibility, parents can repair the interpersonal bridge, which frees their children to move beyond their shame, rage, and the terror of abandonment.

Kaufman elaborates on four reactions by parents which stimulate these feelings of shame and abandonment to the point, at times, of sheer terror for the children. First, these feelings are activated when parents are emotionally unavailable to their children. This can be when parents either inadvertently or more importantly deliberately engage in excessively long periods of silent withdrawal from their children. Children experience these lengthy silences as a refusal to relate to them and tend to believe that this silent withdrawal means that there must be something wrong with them. Second, when parents become overly contemptuous, either facially or verbally, children experience this contemptuousness as a complete rejection of themselves and feel as if they are offensive and disgusting. Third, when parents overtly withdraw their love and affection and prolong this unreasonable behavior toward their children, whatever feelings of abandonment lurk in the children can intensify to the point of sheer terror (Kaufman, 1985). Kaufman also emphasizes the powerful consequences of withholding physical contact with non-verbal children. When parents deliberately or unintentionally withhold a hug or do not physically touch their children when under stress, there has been a rupture in the selfobject tie. This action by parents and caregivers is yet another way of activating or perpetuating feelings of shame and the terror of abandonment in children.

These four recurrent interactions, as well as others that initiate this sequence of shame, abandonment, and terror, make children feel defective and that they are not quite good enough as a person. This feeling of defectiveness forms a foundation around which shame and other feelings about oneself will be experienced. As this belief-affect system gradually recedes from consciousness during the toddler phase when preoperational thinking and symbol formation is consolidated, these feelings of shame, defectiveness, and terror of abandonment become internalized. "In this way, shame becomes basic to the sense of identity" (Kaufman, 1985, p. 66). What creates the power and destructiveness of shame then is that once shame is internalized, shame can be prolonged indefinitely. Shame, in essence, develops a momentum and power of its own that prevents the building of a firm psychological foundation which leaves children vulnerable to further experiences of shame and the terror of abandonment.

Kaufman (1985) also describes how shame is activated when parents experience their children as only an extension of themselves, either to make up for their own deficiencies or to live out their own dreams. Shame is also activated when parents expect their children, consciously or unconsciously, to literally be the parent to their parents. In this case, the natural flow of parents being there primarily for their children is reversed—the children must now tend to the needs of the parents instead. In addition, parents may repeatedly convey to their children that they are never to require anything emotionally from the parents. This attitude in parents "communicates in no uncertain terms that the child should have been born an adult and so must relinquish childhood without ever having had it" (Kaufman, 1985, pp. 46–47).

DISAVOWAL: RETREAT FROM SHAME AND ITS EFFECT ON PSYCHIC DEVELOPMENT

Whether viewed through Kaufman's (1985) shaming system, Miller's (1981, 1983, 1984) description of parents using their children for their own needs, or a self psychological perspective of children being used as selfobjects by parents (Socarides and Stolorow, 1984/85; Ornsteins,

1985; Tolpin, 1987), all of these perspectives highlight how children must change or alter themselves to maintain a relationship with their parents and caregivers. Much like Winnicott's (1960) description of a "false self," this need to hide one's own needs or give up one's feelings to remain connected to parents and caregivers creates, in fact, a self-deception. To maintain this very painful and empty life as a "false self," children must engage in certain primitive defense mechanisms. One such important defense mechanism which allows this "false self" or pathological adaptation to persist, is the extensive use of disavowal.

Disavowal, described by Kohut (1971, 1977, 1984) as a "vertical split," severs one's feelings from the event or experience. There is memory with no feelings. The more encompassing the "false self," due to the children's need to take care of the parents' selfobject needs rather than their own, the greater the split. The result is that whole aspects of the psychological life of children are lost, in essence, they are "split off," like the vertical split described by Kohut.

With an understanding of shame and how it can arouse in children a need to develop a "false self" through disavowal to protect themselves, we can now look at some of the similarities and differences of toddlers and early adolescents.

SIMILARITIES/DIFFERENCES BETWEEN TODDLERS AND EARLY ADOLESCENTS

To simply equate the close connection between the toddler and early adolescent periods in terms of quantum shifts in cognition, heightened egocentrism, strivings for self-integration and issues over shame and abandonment would obscure the important differences between the two phases. However, focusing on the toddler provides a preview of issues crucial to the development and integration of psychic structure in early adolescence.

First, the development of FRIGs, RIGs based on figurative or symbol formation, illuminates how the infant–parent dyad enriches the lives of toddlers as well as provides the foundation for their dynamic unconscious. Second, the struggles for autonomy and self-integration can be observed to stimulate particular primitive defense mechanisms to the newly found strivings of toddlers. Third, the quantum leap in cognitive development from sensorimotor (body) to preoperational (figurative or symbolic) thinking creates cognitive and emotional disequilibriums which parallel this process in early adolescence. In many ways, a gigantic RIG is created based on how parents and caregivers react to their toddlers during such disequilibriums. How toddlers and those around them approach, deal with, and resolve issues and conflicts during this phase provides a glimpse of how early adolescents and those around them will deal with this developmental phase.

One important aspect of this gigantic RIG is the struggles of toddlers for independence. For the first time, they directly challenge parents in order to attain a greater degree of autonomy. This "No" phase, or the "Terrible Two's" as this stage is often called, allows for the strengthening and the securing of self-boundaries. This is accomplished through the capacities of toddlers to establish and test the mastery of their own body through confrontations over control with their parents and caregivers, who function as selfobjects. The need for continued attachments while striving for self-definition creates a state of ambivalence, which is a major hallmark of this phase. The parents' continuing need to fulfill selfobject functions is essential in strengthening their children's self-boundaries. This self-boundary formation is accomplished by confirming selfobjects as allies and by simultaneously confronting selfobjects as antagonists. This interaction helps to develop self-assertion. This increased self-assertion, in turn, mobilizes healthy aggression, which then helps to promote the cohesive strength of self. Occasional scenes at the park, the restaurant, and at the candy or toy store attest to the tug-of-war that is only a preview of what will occur in early adolescence, the next developmental phase that sets up an intense power struggle between children and their parents.

Another important aspect of this gigantic RIG is the newly found capacity for mental representation and symbol formation, which often leads toddlers into more challenging dialectic experiences. On the one hand, there is an enormous expansion of their world while, at the same time, there is a concomitant sense of smallness or shrinking in relationship to their world. The anxiety aroused results in reestablishment of dependency and a demanding type of egocentrism. From both a cognitive and an emotional point of view, the capacity for figurative thinking puts a new burden on the growing youngster, to which s/he responds initially by an increased egocentrism.

As in early adolescence, the quantum leap in cognitive thinking of toddlers leads to a softening of their psychic structure, or a difficulty in maintaining consistency in their set of organizing principles. This difficulty in maintaining an internal sense of consistency, especially under stress, results in major cognitive and emotional disequilibriums. This extreme vulnerability, simultaneously occurring in the midst of this push for autonomy, creates a fragility and a concomitant need for external sources for self-esteem regulation (Greenspan, 1979; Cotton, 1985). As with early adolescents, this need to rely on external sources creates intense ambivalence in toddlers.

Another similarity between toddlers and early adolescents is the various factors that contribute to the development and maintenance of self-esteem regulation during both phases. First, with the widening of their world, toddlers develop a hierarchy of persons and groups who validate their self-esteem. The world of toddlers suddenly expands beyond the immediate world of their parents and now includes siblings and peers. Also at this time, group membership begins to influence their self-esteem. In addition, along with starting to form their gender identity (Stoller, 1968; Tyson, 1982), toddlers also identify themselves as part of a family. "If the gender and family are valued, then the toddler's self-esteem is enhanced" (Cotton, 1985, p. 128).

Second, the issue of competence and being able to master their expanding world is of extreme importance for toddlers. There are a number of new areas of proficiency so that: "The toddler's development of competence is enhanced by the 'elation' which accompanies the experience of newfound motor, cognitive, and language skills" (Cotton, 1985, p. 128).

The last factor which fosters the development of self-esteem regulation, a crucial segment of their set of organizing principles or psychic structure, is the self. At this phase, self-esteem regulation starts to become more dependent on intrapsychic structures with the consolidation of their new cognitive processes. Children continue to construct a sense of self from their multiple life experiences. The integration or connection of these self-experiences develops " . . . an intrapsychic organization of experience that is felt as continuous over time and space, stable and cohesive" (Kohut, 1971, 1972, 1977, quoted in Cotton, 1985, p. 129).

As toddlers consolidate these massive changes and have a sense of a more secure psychic foundation, their extreme vulnerability and need for external support systems diminishes. Parallel to these changes, toddlers move gradually away from being "the center of the universe" (A. Freud, 1936; Schave, 1981, Schave, 1985) to the pre- and post-

Copernican views of the solar system (Ausubel, 1950; Cotton, 1985). In this process of slowly learning that they are a satellite attached to more powerful and competent parents, toddlers begin to incorporate parental qualities, roles, and a sense of power into their developing sense of self. With this growing awareness and acceptance of the importance of their parents as regulators of self-esteem, toddlers are able to maintain their self-esteem more easily during times of stress or vulnerability. The result is a calmer relationship between toddlers and their parents and caregivers.

SELFOBJECT FAILURES: THEIR EFFECT ON PSYCHIC DEVELOPMENT

Tolpin (1987) states that when parents function as selfobjects and consistently fail children, children suffer from what amounts to faults and failings in their own self-maintaining and restoring psychic structure. To protect their faulty self or their sense of impending self-fragmentation, they institute their own pathogenic measures to bolster their failing sense of self. As a result, "sensuality and aggression, and the complex mental processes, including fantasy, already available to two-year-olds, are used to fill in for what is missing from their selfobjects (comfort, stimulation, and enjoyment, etc.). . . . In short, they become 'anal-sadistic' as they try to strengthen themselves and bolster their failing self-esteem and faltering sense of power and efficacy with the lonely satisfaction of isolated infantile sexuality and aggression" (Tolpin, 1987, p. 236). The result is a pathological superstructure that begins to take shape, but which is built over inner states of psychic confusion.

Tolpin (1987) believes that two different, but interrelated, pathological sequences are initiated at this point. First, toddlers experience a collapse of their sense of self as a coherent organization. Various aspects of themselves, such as their sense of initiative, aliveness, vigor, resiliency, and even their senses of continuity, reality, and self-assurance are all affected. Second, without the necessary selfobjects present, children attempt to rely on their own immature resources to reconstitute their sense of self. With limited and immature resources to rely on, children often turn to isolated pleasures. These isolated pleasures, viewed as disintegration products from a self psychological perspective, include infantile sexuality, aggression, and fantasy in a desperate attempt, much like Humpty-Dumpty, of putting themselves back together again. The end result of these two sequences, the disruption of cohesion and the defense against the disruption, lead to a broad spectrum of self-disturbances, including narcissistic and borderline disorders.

OEDIPAL PHASE: PREOPERATIONAL THINKING, INTUITIVE PHASE

Cotton (1985) sees continual successful mastery of events and situations as developing more complex structures, which do not mature until late adolescence. The hierarchy of valuable parts of the sense of self of preschoolers, such as their mode of self-conceptualization, competencies, identifications with parental qualities, roles, and values, continue to be integrated. These older children still define themselves by overt aspects of themselves and by the intense feelings about good and bad that they develop during this period. The magical thinking, lack of introspection, and blurred concepts between fantasy and reality cause the self-worth of these young children to still be extremely vulnerable to everyday experiences including how their parents feel about them.

In the continued development of healthy self-esteem regulation, the sense of self depends upon the quality and intensity of children's reactions to the inevitable discrepancies between the actual and ideal self. To maintain a positive sense of themselves, children must return to a state of positive self-esteem in a reasonable time without dwelling on failure, disappointment, and rejection. "Parental mediation of the preschool child's initially intense reactions to failure and rejection help shape more emotionally tolerable reactions" (Cotton, 1985, p. 134). This view is very similar to Demos (1982, 1983, 1984), Stern (1985), and Demos and Kaplan (1986).

LATENCY: CONCRETE OPERATIONAL THINKING

According to Cotton (1985), by the time children enter grammar school, the three sources of self-esteem have become integrated. The self continues to act as a selective filter. Latency children are still highly dependent on the praise of others, particularly of persons whom they highly value. However, for some children, intense negative patterns have already become an established part of their world. These children are unable to restore positive feelings about themselves, "regardless of the nature or extent of environmental support for developing competence or identification with positive models. The self has become a filter which selectively values new experiences because they validate a negative self-image which has been formed out of past experiences'' (Cotton, 1985, p. 136).

Cotton views latency children as believing that ''the ultimate truth about the self is to be found in some external source'' (Rosenberg, 1979, quoted in Cotton, 1985, p. 136). Thus latency-age children, much like early adolescents, seek out information from others because they believe valued adults have a more accurate view of them than they have. Parents still have a tremendous influence, so even in the presence of competence, acceptance among peers, and approval from teachers, the absence of approval and praise from parents often results in a sense of poor or low self-esteem. Examination of the family constellation of such children often reveals ''an impaired mother—or father–child relation-ship with excessive criticism, unreasonable expectations, or marked neglect of the child's psychological needs'' (Cotton, 1985, p. 136). At this age, moral decisions become increasingly important to self-esteem regulation. ''Whether a child can live up to his moral decisions has a major impact on self-esteem regulation in latency'' (Cotton, 1985, p. 137). For a positive self-esteem, children need to feel that they can live up to their own standards, modeled after parents, teachers and other cultural guides.

The phase of latency allows for the relative consolidation of a set of organizing principles or psychic structure that remains stable until early adolescence. Hopefully, with good-enough parenting, and the laying down of predominately positive FRIGs, latency children will develop a growing sense of self with a firm base of self-esteem fostered by their parents. Parents, who continue to provide selfobject functions on a more mature level as the cognition and emotional levels of their children become more sophisticated, help consolidate a stronger sense of self and a stronger set of organizing principles or the psychic structure.

TRANSITIONS FROM CHILDHOOD TO EARLY ADOLESCENCE

We believe that the formation of FRIGs, built upon the earlier nonverbal RIGs, along with adequate self-esteem regulation, and an average ex-pectable environment (Hartmann, 1958) provide an increasingly solid sense for toddlers. This sense of self is what provides a smooth template for movement into grammar school. Unfortunately, some parents, who themselves are struggling with issues of being afraid of the world, feeling out of control, or lost, experience their children's need for self-differentiation with trepidation and panic. However, the next time these problems arise is in early adolescence, when issues of separation from the family are again intensified.

5

The Center of the Universe: The Affective Life of the Early Adolescent

THE DEVELOPMENTAL TASKS OF EARLY ADOLESCENCE

One of the crucial developmental tasks of early adolescence is self-integration. Because early adolescents, like toddlers, are seeking self-integration, many of the cognitive and emotional developmental tasks of the early adolescent phase can be viewed as developmentally similar to that of the toddler phase. Just as the quantum leap in cognitive functioning from sensorimotor learning to preoperational thinking sets the tone for the toddler phase, the cognitive quantum leap from concrete operational thinking to formal operational thinking sets the tone for early adolescence. The difficulties or turbulences of both phases are brought on by cognitive and emotional disequilibriums which strongly influence how self-experiences are integrated and processed.

In early adolescence, the foundation of self-esteem regulation, one's set of organizing principles, or psychic structure, is due to these psychological disequilibriums and oftentimes the arousal of shame or a sense of impending self-fragmentation. These psychological disequilibriums also result in an intensified need for greater external support to maintain psychic equilibrium. When the unpredictability of external supports are intertwined with the change in cognitive processes, this inevitably results in an intensification, as well as, a volatility and instability in the affect states of early adolescents. This intensification results in a greater need for parents to continue to function as selfobjects in their roles as modulators, regulators, and facilitators of the varying states of mind of their early adolescents.

Intensification of this need for parents to function as selfobjects is similar, in many ways, to the need of toddlers, whose strivings for self-integration are also coupled with a concomitant increased dependency. These struggles over dependency by both age groups create a similar increased ambivalence toward parents and significant others.

Yet, the differences between toddlers and early adolescents are remarkably distinct. Early adolescents not only think that they can exist without parents, but they actually believe that they have the capacity to be psychologically and physiologically independent. Their feelings and cognitive capacities are quite different from the feelings and cognitive capacities of toddlers, who are totally dependent on parents and caregivers for their psychological and physical well-being.

It is essential to understand that part of the task of early adolescence includes developing new and higher levels of psychic organization in order to deal with their expanding world. In addition, higher levels of psychic organization allow for further affect regulation and affect integration. In other words, psychological disequilibriums result in a number of potentially positive and negative consequences.

First, as suggested, self-esteem regulation becomes unstable due to the softening of the psychic structure of early adolescents. Early adolescents lack the ability to maintain psychic equilibrium, particularly during periods of intense stress or intense affects, without relying more intensively on external support systems. Reliance on these external supports leaves early adolescents vulnerable to the availability and responsiveness of these external support systems as selfobjects. Second, as a result of this softening or fluidity of their psychic structure, early adolescents have an increased ability to alter their set of organizing principles, hence, the potential for fostering further affect integration. The ability to alter, or at least to effect deeply embedded patterns, allows for the possibility of repairing and restructuring previous misattunements, RIGs or FRIGs. Third, if this greater fluidity in their set of organizing principles or psychic structure is coupled with a continued or sudden lack of appropriate affect attunement by selfobjects, the result can lead to even more extreme emotionality, psychic pain, and a further intensification of misattunements. These misattunements then foster the laying down of new negative FRIGs. These negative FRIGs, especially if formed over previously negative or unstable RIGs, result in a very fragile psychological foundation for early adolescents. In turn, the perpetuation or creation of this very fragile foundation leaves early adolescents continually vulnerable to external pressures, struggling with difficulties in self-esteem regulation, and fighting intense fears about the unpredictable and frightening world about them. The outcome of this psychological vulnerability, whether positive or negative, will depend on the capacity of early adolescents and the availability of their parents to develop and to maintain meaningful selfobject relationships.

Additionally, the increased cognitive capacity which fosters self-integration creates another dialectic for early adolescents. While curiosity about their world allows for feelings of strength and expansiveness, concomitantly, this expansiveness creates a sense of shrinking and extreme vulnerability, as well as an increased need for closeness. The antecedents of the strivings for this psychological autonomy begin with the first steps early adolescents took as young children in their movement toward independent play. Richmond and Sklansky emphasize this connection between toddlers and early adolescents by stating, "just as a sensitive mother tries to facilitate independent play in her child, so too should sensitive parents help their adolescent in the move toward autonomy" (Richmond and Sklansky, 1984, p. 115). These authors find, both in the play of toddlers and in the self-seriousness of adolescents, a determined assertion of a deeply felt right to be, to behave the way one feels and to decide for oneself. Anything that is experienced as interfering with their autonomous strivings is perceived by them as threatening their core sense of being in their "search for self."

THE STRUGGLE FOR INDEPENDENCE: ITS EFFECT ON PSYCHIC DEVELOPMENT

What is the effect of this greater push for autonomy? Recently, our society unfortunately appears to view early adolescents more and more as young adults (Elkind, 1981, 1984). In our opinion, the reality is that the striving for self-integration, when coupled with the cognitive, emotional, physical, pubertal, and social changes of this age group, creates volatile states of mind, which do not lend themselves to allowing early adolescents to be treated like adults. When their lack of life-experiences and resulting immaturity are coupled with their propensity to rapidly shifting states of mind, they do not have the solid psychic foundation, or set of organizing principles firmly formed enough to assume the functions of young adults, no matter how mature they may try to act or appear.

During times of stress, due to the changes in their cognitive capacities, they put a greater reliance on external sources of support (Cotton, 1985). Thus, paradoxically, at a time when early adolescents are striving to reach independence and self-sufficiency, their need for dependency is inherently increased. Unfortunately, and far too often, early adolescents are left alone, unprotected, and overwhelmed by the myriad of stimuli and changes. The protective umbrella joyfully and energetically provided by parents and caregivers for their toddlers is no longer an option. With young adolescents capable of looking, acting, and at times demanding to be treated like adults, they are often unwisely left to fend for themselves, as if they are older adolescents or young adults. However, "latch key" early adolescents are just as isolated, if not more so, than younger children.

ISSUES OF SHAME: THE CORE AFFECT OF EARLY ADOLESCENCE

The Parental Dilemma

Underneath the bravado of autonomy and independence of most early adolescents lies a fragile self-structure. Shame and other related phenomena, such as humiliation, mortification, remorse, apathy, and embarrassment, are easily activated. These affects and the struggles with self-esteem regulation are the core issues of this phase and predominate in the psychic life of early adolescents (Morrison, 1984). For example, parents merely looking at their early adolescents often send them into a reactive rage. This narcissistic rage to such a seemingly nonthreatening situation—parents looking at their children—is the result of early adolescents experiencing their parents as overly judgmental, condemning, humiliating, and ultimately creating intense states of shame. Kaufman's (1985) triad of fear, hurt, and rage to the experiencing of this shame predominates in their fluctuating states of mind. In addition, the primitive moral judgments of early adolescents, "an eye for an eye," particularly when experiencing shame from a primary narcissistic wound, demand revenge and immediate retaliation. This retaliation is often too much for parents to comprehend or tolerate. There are no white flags of peace unless parents offer unconditional surrender. Every slight, every put-down, or every alleged attack which stimulates shame must be responded to in kind by early adolescents. Never before nor ever again will parents feel so vulnerable to the rejection or attack from their children. With the immediacy and intensity of such explosiveness, it is understandable that the unresolved issues of parents to their own adolescence are reactivated in these daily interactions with their young teenagers.

Even parents with a solid psychic foundation cannot help feeling at times that they are on a roller coaster. Parents with their own unresolved adolescence are even more vulnerable and threatened by the intensity and unpredictability of their early adolescents. As a consequence of this volatility, emotional support is essential for parents as well.

Cohen and Weissman (1984) and Cohen, Cohler, and Weissman (1984) emphasize the concept of parental alliance, which is the ability of parents to work harmoniously together during this developmental phase. The parental alliance provides the basis for consistency and support not only for the parents, but also for their early adolescents. Cohen and Weissman state that in families with effective parenting alliances, there is a freedom to experiment with a wide variety of newly acquired capabilities supported by the child–coparent triad. As a consequence, this type of mutually supportive parental alliance makes this phase of early adolescence more tolerable and rewarding.

Parents, who are not able to support each other, or single parents, are often left feeling alone, exposed, vulnerable, attacked, and humiliated. Even the most psychologically intact parents find themselves at times wanting to retaliate toward their early adolescents. Sometimes parents suddenly find themselves saying or doing things in retaliation, much to their surprise. Only moments later, they experience their young teenager countering the retaliation, fleeing the situation in tears, or responding with a deadly silence because of an increased sense of shame, fear, hurt, and rage. It is obvious that the continued parental capacity to remain affectively attuned during these moments lessens the frequency and intensity of the arousal of shame and related affects in both their early adolescents and themselves. This capacity to remain affectively attuned in turn strongly influences the previous FRIGs of their early adolescents as well as their sense of self-worth, self-esteem, and their development of a solid set of organizing principles or psychic structure.

There are a variety of different reactions that parents may engage in when confronted with such attacks over self-integration by their early adolescents. For some parents, who could not deal well with the growing independence of their toddlers, the battles over power and control not only persist, but are intensified during this developmental phase. These negative parental reactions and interactions remain to form a new layer of FRIGs or a higher level of organizing principles in their early adolescents that again reactivates and reinforces the arousal of shame and abandonment for such strivings of autonomy.

However, there are some parents, who, despite difficulties with their children as toddlers, are able to respond more appropriately to their early adolescents. The ability of these parents to relate differently this time to the growing needs of their early adolescents for autonomy allows for the altering and the modifying of new FRIGs and new ways of adapting.

There are also a number of parents who have performed quite competently and who have been affectively attuned to their developing children. However, because of situational stress from the death of a spouse, a severe medical or psychiatric illness, a divorce, or other difficulties, these parents experience intense struggles over separation and independence with their early adolescents. A stronger or more available parenting alliance would allow for a smoother transition through this developmental phase.

However, no matter how secure the parents, no matter how stable the parental alliance, the movements away from home by early adolescents threaten the self-esteem of parents which may arouse intense narcissistic vulnerabilities. In spite of the upheavals, parents must recognize and support the growing needs of their early adolescents. For overprotective parents, the beginning movement by their early adolescents out of the home is experienced as an enormous loss. For parents who have needed their children to function as their own selfobject, the loss is even more catastrophic. Many times these parents are "fighting for their own psychological lives" in their battles to keep the heart and soul of their early adolescents at home. Unfortunately early adolescents with this type of family structure may experience the family as suffocating and they may respond by trying to cut themselves off totally from their parents.

One way early adolescents will attempt to compensate for this loss of their parents or appropriately attuned selfobjects is to find, within their peer groups, necessary and convenient selfobjects to merge with in order to foster a more secure sense of self. Kohut's (1971, 1977, 1984) descriptions of an alter ego or twinship are examples of this intense need for a mirror image of oneself. At the other extreme are underinvolved parents who are too busy or too detached because of their own lives, problems, or fears. In this type of family structure, early adolescents are left with an affect hunger and a need to find selfobjects outside of the house to help contain their tremendous sense of deprivation and to attempt to undo the intense feelings of shame. For both of these groups, the answer, unfortunately, is often found in peer groups that encourage an antiauthority attitude and the use of sex, drugs, and various forms of self-destructive activities.

THE RETREAT FROM SHAME

As stated previously, the quantum leap in cognition, which occurs at the beginning of early adolescence, results in the fluidity of psychic structure and an inability to maintain a psychic equilibrium during stressful situations without external support. This instability in their organizing principles, coupled with the assault of multiple stimuli—puberty, struggles with parents and authority, the influence of peers, school, sex, drugs, and AIDS—causes early adolescents to no longer feel safe in their expanding world. The protective umbrella of earlier years has disappeared. The result, for most early adolescents, is a strategic retreat to a safer psychological world. Even affectively attuned parents are often shut out. With these various psychological disequilibriums, the rapid shifts in states of mind, and the resulting sense of their affective lives being out of control, early adolescents increasingly use massive disavowal to split off emotions from their psychic life. This split is particularly preponderant around the affect of shame. The use of disavowal (Basch, 1983, 1985) allows for the disconnection of emotions from events and memories. The memories and events are there, but there is a total absence of any feelings.

The disconnection caused by disavowal has been described by Kohut (1971, 1977, 1984), as a vertical split. This vertical split is quite different from the horizontal split, or repression, so well described in classical literature. The more early adolescents struggle to diminish the overwhelming affect storms that swirl around them, the greater their need to escape through disavowal. The psychological result for early adolescents is a loss of contact with their psychic life, in essence, with their inner world of feelings and thoughts—their dynamic unconscious. With this unconscious decision to treat an experience as if it does not matter, the immediate benefit is that children, early adolescents, or even adults avoid the affect experiences that they fear. Thus, when parents attempt to be affectively attuned by asking their early adolescent how they are, rather than a reply implying comfort with the interaction as in the past, the reply is often a short, "Fine," "No," or "None of your business!" Already disillusioned with their parents, early adolescents delve further into a world of secrecy. This secrecy is often a desperate attempt to try to hide their sense of massive vulnerability and fear of shame from the outside world, as well as ultimately from their own inner life.

EMPATHY: THE VEHICLE FOR COMMUNICATION WITHIN THE FAMILY

What often gets lost in the struggle with these intense states of vulnerability and shame is empathy. As a result, empathy, the essential vehicle for communication among family members, may not be available to maintain family ties. Our definition of empathy follows the comments of Ornstein (1981), who quotes Norman L. Paul: "Empathy . . . presupposes the existence of the object as a separate individual entitled to his own feelings, ideas, and emotional history. The empathizer makes no judgments about what the other *should* feel, but solicits the expression of whatever he *does* feel, and for brief periods experiences these feelings as his own" (her italics) (Paul, 1970, p. 341, quoted in A. Ornstein, 1981, p. 448).

Ornstein, elaborating on the concept of empathy between children and parents, states:

Each child creates his own mother and father, and the responses of the parents become specially 'dovetailed' to the specific need of the particular child. *Therein lies the essence of parental empathy: that the parent does not respond out of her own needs, nor in keeping with prescriptions as to how to be a good parent, but that his/her responses are determined by the needs of the particular child at a particular time in the child's life* (her italics) (A. Ornstein, 1981, p. 448).

Contained within this quote lie the seeds of the loss of empathy in the interaction between early adolescents and their parents. Most psychiatric literature views the struggles between early adolescents and their parents as based on the reemergence of the oedipal conflict. Blos (1967, 1970, 1979) has one of the most detailed descriptions of the movement through this process. Marohn (1977, 1979, 1981), in his reviews of adolescent psychic development, has bridged classical theory and self psychology, emphasizing the struggle over separation.

Within our developmental perspective, the main focus is the interactive process between early adolescents and their parents. This interactive process is based on several components: the various RIGs and FRIGs, the temperament of early adolescents, the ability of the parents to facilitate self-integration, and the struggle experienced by their early adolescents over their disengagement from their parents. In fact, the capacity to remain empathic is based on the ability of parents to deal with their own struggles. These struggles include their own strivings toward autonomy and self-integration which are based on the interactions of parents with their own archaic selfobjects. This entire complex of interactions is based on a supraordinate RIG of what occurred during the toddler phase.

Because we do not view the struggles of early adolescents as exclusively an intrapsychic struggle over sexual feelings, we believe that parents play a critical and pivotal role in their resolution. When parents are able to accept the competitiveness and assertiveness of their early adolescents, this capacity facilitates their striving for self-differentiation and individuality. When separation difficulties centering round sexuality and aggression become too intensified, the resulting dynamics are like the sexualized struggles so often described in the psychiatric literature for narcissistic and borderline psychopathology, including a focus on sexualized fantasies or acting out promiscuity.

Young females' struggles with their mothers, rather than due to the fear of homosexual engulfment, appear, from the authors' viewpoint, to be more involved with the previous RIGs and the pattern of the infant–parent dyad during the toddler phase. Mothers who can comfortably appreciate the growing sexuality and femininity of their daughters, and fathers who can also appreciate and enjoy their growing sense of being young women allow their daughters to feel like separate individuals. This interaction also allows for the conscious and unconscious development of what classical literature calls an ego ideal. Traditional theory views the development of the superego and ego ideal of females as less formed and weaker than those of males because of a lack of resolution of the oedipal complex. We view the development of the superego and ego ideal as based on the interactions with parents. In particular, mothers who foster and encourage self-integration allow their daughters to develop a deep sense of self-confidence. However, when mothers require their daughters to behave certain ways or maintain a connection that stifles individuality, the resulting psychic structure is similar to what has traditionally been written about in classical literature.

In our perspective, the struggle between young teenagers and parents is based on their need for individuality which may be extremely difficult to act upon. There are several ways to compensate for the ambivalent and painful loss of parents as selfobjects. One way is the attachment to or idealization of other adults in a renewed search for mirroring and idealization. For example, the opportunity of junior high school students to find a teacher who recreates that "gleam in the parent's eyes" experienced many years ago as younger children is a precious find. Another important way to compensate for the selfobject losses is the development of a twinship with peers. Girls, in particular, find friends who wear the same things, say the same things, and do the same things.

Another way of compensating for the loss in mirroring and idealizing includes finding music and movie stars to fulfill these functions. Unfortunately many early adolescents with severe self-esteem problems find themselves compelled to engage in more desperate measures. They often turn toward older adolescents who have an antiauthority and antischool attitude as a way to avoid dealing with their own empty and isolated existences. All too often, many early adolescents we see in our office, or particularly by therapists who work in psychiatric hospitals or residential placements, choose drugs and sexuality as the pathways in their struggle to avoid feeling isolated and intensely depressed and empty—the "black hole" (Grotstein, 1988).

PEERS AS SELFOBJECTS

Besides pursuing new relationships with adults outside of the family, the "search for self" by early adolescents continues with increased involvement with peers and peer groups. Peer groups become more important as parents lose touch with their early adolescents. Not only do parents often feel alienated from the younger generation, but early adolescents can also experience this psychological disconnection as an acute loss. Through peer groups, early adolescents can reexperience the confirmation of phase-appropriate grandiosity. They can also experience the potential for developing idealizing selfobjects through relationship with group idols. "When internalized, the latter relation strengthens the pole of values and ideals of the bipolar self and may well set the direction for choice of vocation and mate" (Wolf, 1980, p. 127–128).

Shame remains a very important dynamic even in peer relationships. The fear of being shamed or humiliated is motivated by the same dynamic as the extreme egocentrism and sensitivities to self-criticism that early adolescents experienced with their parents. Their tendency to react to the imaginary audience is present in relationships with peers. Here too, the power of the imaginary audience results in a sense of being on a darkened stage with bright spotlights always focused on themselves, never being able to see the audience, but always waiting for the disapproval, crude remarks, judgments, and put-downs of their peers.

This extreme sensitivity and vulnerability to shame and humiliation by peers is handled in a number of ways. Most early adolescents find peers who share certain similarities, including the same sex. Similarity between peers can also include the creation of a uniform or dress code as well as rules for greetings, what games can be played, or what topics can be discussed. A "language" is created by these peer groups with all the special idiosyncratic sayings that function to replace the protective umbrella previously provided by parents. Through this sense of similarity, in particular the oneness provided by twinship, peer groups provide the sense of safety from the rest of the world which parents provided earlier.

This need for a twinship, alterego, or oneness has negative effects as well. The harshness, extreme prejudices, and the cruel, sadistic behaviors of this age group can be merciless to "outsiders." The power of exclusion and the resultant intense reactions are most evident in early adolescents. For example, effeminate behavior (or what a particular group might define as effeminate or homosexual-like actions, behaviors, or speech) creates a great deal of anxiety, often unconsciously. The reaction of peer groups to these individuals is often not only avoidance, but outright ostracism. Early adolescents react to these individuals, or any individuals as if they are different, as if they have the black plague— they must be avoided at all costs or "something deadly will happen."

Besides the use of peer groups for self-affirmation and self-esteem regulation, there are a variety of more troublesome adaptations to the loss of protection from parents. Certain early adolescents who are starved for attention and acceptance can become trend setters as a way of coping with their struggles with poor self-esteem and anxiety. Trend-setters are often seen by others as secure, confident, and "with it." These early adolescents, underneath their perfect exteriors, can be just as confused and just as anxious as most other early adolescents. However, early adolescents with these types of underlying problems take on the role of "the leader" in order to use their position of power to manipulate, control, and at times emotionally destroy others as a way of feeling "on top of things" and in control of themselves.

Whenever there is an "in crowd," there must also be "the others." "The others" are often early adolescents who are even more insecure and frightened. These "other" early adolescents are accepted as part of the group only on the whim of "the leader." Once in, "the others" must dutifully follow the orders and dictates of "the leader" and the appointed group members. These young teenagers tolerate being unmercifully controlled, attacked, shamed, and humiliated by the leader and group because of their fear of ostracism, banishment, and isolation if they protest. This ensuing loneliness, which is experienced as extremely frightening and, in turn, intolerable, results in these insecure early adolescents feeling that they must submit to the abuses of the group. They feel and believe that they have no choice. When confronted with the dilemma of being a member of the group and being shamed and humiliated or being banished from the group, which will activate feelings of being abandoned and isolated, the shame is tolerated. The fear of experiencing the "black hole" is postponed for a short while until the "next time."

An illustration of the power of the "in crowd" is described in the following example of "sadistic treatment" given to a very attractive, but very insecure eighth grader. This young female adolescent felt lost and adrift due to a terrible home situation, academic problems at her school, and fears of nobody liking her. Specifically, this early adolescent was always fearful of being rejected, in particular by a group of girls she admired. She was so desperate to be a member of this "in crowd" that she allowed the group of girls to trim her shoulder length hair. Predictably, not only did the group cut off her long hair, but they butchered it, leaving her to face the scorn and humiliation of the group, as well as the rest of her class and the entire high school. In spite of this cruel treatment, this eighth grade girl continued to stay with these girls. She felt that she could not exist without the approval from this group which meant that she continued to allow them to openly humiliate her. The cost of humiliation for continued acceptance into the group was for her far less a price to pay than the cost of feeling rejected and having to face the depression, isolation, and emptiness of her life—the "black hole."

Early adolescents who are "different" are also confronted with the spector of continual shame, rejection, and isolation by peers. Young adolescents with medical problems and physical handicaps, who are always struggling as they compare themselves with what they could be with what they are, must all wrestle with feeling different, being picked on, and being targeted for the scorn of those too insecure to feel comfortable around them.

Even nonvisible problems, such as learning disabilities, present difficulties. Self-esteem problems are characteristic of early adolescents with learning disabilities as they find themselves continually falling behind or struggling when other students seem to be dealing easily with their academics. The egocentrism which creates the "imaginary audience" and the comparison of what could be with what is, is fostered by the emergence of formal operational thinking. This egocentrism forces early adolescents to look at their failures and shortcomings. The issue of shame is even more overwhelming for these young teenagers, particularly when attending "special" classes or having to leave regular classes for "tutoring." These early adolescents often feel as if they are walking down a long hallway, wearing a dunce cap while other students are laughing, jeering, and taunting them all the way out the door.

A recent issue that evokes intense reactions in young teenagers involves the AIDS epidemic and the fear some early adolescents have of "being contaminated." The unfortunate national headlines of junior high school students stricken with AIDS being treated by their fellow students, their parents, and even some of their teachers, as if they had leprosy, has occurred all too often in a number of communities. Reflecting the greater tolerance for differences in older adolescents was the return of a student with AIDS into a high school setting. Although attending high school in a different city, this student was readily accepted by his classmates, unlike at his previous junior high school only a year before.

Sexuality: Its Role in Psychic Development

In early adolescence, sexuality is often far from the genital sexuality of the older adolescent. Although sexual interest and curiosity is emerging for many early adolescents, the authors do not believe that sexuality is the main emotional or cognitive concern for most early adolescents. When sexuality and aggression predominate they are primarily viewed as a product of the breakdown in selfobject functioning early in life (Tolpin, 1987). For many early adolescents, the only way to escape the absence of affect attunement and the lack of a holding environment at home is to escape into the world of sexuality. Females, in particular, are often less interested in sex, yearning instead for physical contact and craving someone to hug them. These young adolescents merely want a teddy bear to soothe them and momentarily cover up the emptiness of the "black hole." This need for a teddy bear is often an attempt to take the place of their missing parents who are unavailable to act as modulators, containers, and facilitators of their overwhelming and oftentimes depressive affects.

Female early adolescents who need to believe that they are in fact much older have a tendency to find an older male for a companion. The older teenager is not only more sexually mature, but if struggling with their own problems with poor self-esteem and faltering psychic structures, these males may also use sexuality as a way to avoid their own "black hole" or empty depression and isolation. For many early adolescent males, the macho image of "making it" with a female is only a desperate attempt to cover up their narcissistic vulnerability and the false doubts which lurk just below the surface.

Our point of view does not exclude sexuality as developmentally important for this age group. The authors agree with Kaufman (1985) who suggests that it is vital for early adolescents to have the affirmation of their emerging sexuality from the opposite-sex parent. These interactions help develop a sense of pride in their sexuality and in themselves. This greater sense of self-worth allows the building of a solid foundation, a sense of comfort about their sexuality, which makes later relationships more satisfying and gratifying. "What is needed is for the opposite sex parent simply to *accept* the boy's or the girl's practicing and to *admire* his emerging masculinity or her emerging femininity . . . In my view, such 'complementarity' is a form of affirmation of the child's or adolescent's emerging manliness or womanliness" (his italics) (Kaufman, 1985, p. 63).

When parents are unable to openly acknowledge and value this aspect of their early adolescents' sense of self, shame is quickly activated and is experienced as a crushing blow to the early adolescents' emerging sense of sensuality and sexuality. Shame again plays an enormous part when fathers pull away from their daughters, because of their own struggles over sexuality.

Even more difficult for early adolescent females are fathers who, due to problems in their marriages, will use their daughters as sexual objects and replacements for their lack of emotional and sexual intimacy with their wives. The sexualization of the father-daughter relationship sets up a potentially life-long, self-destructive pattern of daughters giving up their identity to please males. The extreme of this abuse, incest, destroys any sense of trust with a father or father figure. This basic betrayal by a father or other male forces the young female to give up her own needs totally at the great psychic cost of the development of a "false self." When this occurs, daughters are left feeling overwhelmed, ashamed, emotionally empty, and abandoned. In addition, with the integration of their sense of sensuality and sexuality severely damaged, their later capacity for sexual and sensual pleasure is likewise severely disrupted.

Having given the reader what we hope is a comprehensive view of the affective life and the struggles of early adolescence, we will next discuss what often occurs when there are chronic selfobject failures at home and make some generalizations about the treatment of early adolescents.

CONSEQUENCES OF SELFOBJECT FAILURES IN EARLY ADOLESCENCE

Early adolescents are subject to a variety of emotional problems that are specific to this age group. Although many of their problems are multifaceted, they derive basically from misattunements which develop from chronic selfobject failures. When these failures and their ensuing misattunements begin at birth, more severe psychopathology or developmental arrests are created during early adolescence than when selfobject failures begin at later developmental levels. Likewise, failures that are more sustained or intense will generally create more severe psychopathology.

These misattunements can have varying consequences, which are partly dependent on each infant's temperament and the innate capacity to interact with parents, as well as the parental capacity to be emotionally present and affectively attuned. When coupled with the impact of environmental stresses, such as a mother's or father's daily emotional availability, one can see that selfobject ties can become disturbed for a variety of reasons. Indeed, selfobject failures are a complicated issue, which makes general statements about causality and psychopathology in early adolescence quite difficult. Recognizing the multiple variables present in any situation, even in selfobject failures, the remainder of this chapter will review what we see as some of the major emotional problems for early adolescents, particularly those seen in an outpatient setting.

A valuable way to look at psychopathology in early adolescence is in terms of a continuum ranging from internal conflicts to externalized acting-out or behavior disorders. Conflicts are internalized or externalized based on how young teenagers organize their thoughts and their feelings, in essence, their set of organizing principles and their psychic structure. Early adolescents who internalize their problems and who become withdrawn and self-critical are very different from those early adolescents who externalize their problems and act them out. Young teenagers who internalize their problems and struggles are always worried about being judged and of not being perfect enough. They are always setting limits for themselves. On the other hand, acting-out young adolescents often require outside agencies to set limits or render consequences for behaviors that neither they nor their families are able to contain, modulate, or control.

The Internalization of Conflict and Structure

Early adolescents who internalize their problems tend to be struggling with Narcissistic Personality Disorders as described by Kohut and Wolf (1978). These symptoms include a sense of enfeeblement or serious distortion of the self. While this state of mind is often temporary, symptoms such as hypochondriasis, hypersensitivity to slights, or a lack of gusto may appear. These symptoms are more directly related to the psychological state of mind of early adolescents rather than to their actions or interactions. With these early adolescents, a number of underlying dynamics tend to be rather constant. Primarily, there is difficulty with their self-esteem regulation. Early adolescents who have internalized conflicts have severe concerns about other people's reactions and constantly worry about being accepted and being liked. The activation of shame is quite prominent in this group of early adolescents.

There are several ways in which the internalization of this type of psychopathology appears (Burch, 1985). First, there are the "perfect" early adolescents who outwardly appear to be doing quite well. In fact, these young teenagers usually do extremely well in school and are often referred to as "overachievers." They are obedient, both with their parents and other adults. They can often be compliant with their friends. If they are involved with peers that are not as creative, intelligent, or social, they in essence become the leader as well. In these types of relationships, they can take care of or protect their friends. Often these early adolescents seem to "survive" early adolescence because they "look so good" and no one sees them as having any problems. If emotional problems do become apparent, whether in junior high school or later in high school, it is due to an intensification of internalized stresses or pressures. These stresses can be related to excessive academic pressures, problems with peers, or family pressures. When these "perfect" early adolescents "fall apart," they often become overly anxious, withdraw from competitive activities, or become phobic. The phobic nature of their behavior may be in terms of school or of not being able to visit or sleep over at friends' houses. Later in life, these teenagers may have considerable problems with self-esteem regulation and difficulties asserting themselves with friends or new situations. They will also tend to ruminate or obsess whether people like them and will continually wonder if they have done the correct thing. Shame, or rather the avoidance of shame, is a powerful motivator. They are constantly worried about doing poorly, of being shamed, but their use of disavowal is much less extensive than early adolescents who externalize their problems.

Another type of early adolescent with similar emotional psychodynamics is the "withdrawn" teenager. These early adolescents tend to fade into the background. They may not always be as intellectually driven as the "perfect" early adolescents, but they are just as terrified of people not liking them and of being shamed. Their self-esteem is extremely shaky, which results in their continual need to believe that no one likes them. They are afraid to get close to their peers. They are also frightened by authority figures and are reluctant to get close to teachers and other adults. In both cases, shame is an important element in their feeling a need to withdraw and hide from people, peers and adults alike. Because these early adolescents are so quiet and nondisruptive, they are often left alone by families and school alike.

There is a deep and pervasive sense that they are not important in the lives of other people. These early adolescents are continually worried about being caught and being shamed and humiliated because they are too dumb, too insecure, and too shy. While they have good friends, they cannot trust that anyone can value them. They are worried that they say "really dumb things" to their friends. Even in class these early adolescents tend to sit back and watch. They are too afraid to ask questions as all too often someone has laughed at them or made a remark that in their mind means that they are "different" from everyone else in a negative way. Ultimately, they believe that no one understands them. Because they do so well, everyone takes it for granted that everything is "okay." Unless there are serious incidents or external problems that attract the attention of their families or school authorities, these students often "slip through the cracks." They usually manifest emotional problems later in life with a shyness that leaves them terrified of the world and new situations, and an inability to stand up for their rights. As adults, they tend to have a difficult time acknowledging the extent of their problems because they must face their shame and their sense of underlying defectiveness. Having to explore their sense of defectiveness is usually quite terrifying. Often these early adolescents enter psychotherapy as adults because of phobic disorders, frustrations with relationships, and social isolation.

Passive–aggressive early adolescents have dynamics similar to the "perfect" or "withdrawn" teenagers. They are different because of a greater underlying hostility toward others. Most often, they are unable to deal openly with their anger or other feelings. They tend to go "underground," and engage in "guerilla warfare." Their sense of shame is much greater and they use disavowal to a greater degree in order to cover up their struggles and their fears of having to deal with their overwhelming problems. These early adolescents are difficult to work with in psychotherapy both at this age and as adults.

The Externalization of Conflict and Structure

Early adolescents who externalize their conflicts would closely fit our description of the Narcissistic Behavior Personality as described by Kohut and Wolf (1978) or borderline early adolescents (Masterson, 1968, 1981; Rinsley, 1980). These early adolescents have greater problems with self-esteem and self-esteem regulation. They also have greater difficulties with other aspects of their psychic structure and their RIGs and FRIGs are much more chaotic.

As a result, these early adolescents have a more pervasive sense that selfobjects will not be consistently available to provide the care and comfort they crave. This feeling, which goes back to early infancy, leaves a deep and longstanding depression described by these early adolescents as a "black hole." No matter how they try to fill up their inner emptiness, the "black hole" sucks everything up—there never is enough. The feeling states activated by the "black hole" are intolerable. As a result, these early adolescents are unable to control either the internal emptiness or the ensuing rage at their parents for being unavailable as "good enough" selfobjects. Likewise, they have greater problems with peers and school. In school, they tend to act out their fears and difficulties by either playing the class clown or by being the defiant and aggressive student.

More severe acting out has been described as borderline psychopathology. Palombo (1987) believes there is a neurocognitive deficit in all borderline children. His views could be extrapolated to early adolescents as well. Another well-known author on adolescents, Masterson (1968), stated in his original book, *Treatment of the Borderline Adolescent* that every borderline adolescent has a borderline mother. In his most recent book, Masterson (1981) alters this stance by acknowledging that other factors contribute to the genesis of borderline adolescents. Neurocognitive deficits are listed as one of the factors considered in the genesis of borderline early adolescents. Neurocognitive deficits can be in the parents, the early adolescent, or in both.

This neurocognitive deficit results in an interactive style which does not allow parents to understand or to respond appropriately to their developing children. Likewise, early adolescents are often not able to take in and integrate the appropriate selfobject functioning of their parents. As a result, the multiple misattunements and selfobject failures lead to the development of a pervasive sense of emptiness, of no one being there. This sense of internal emptiness, the "black hole," results in a rage that is very hard to control. These early adolescents engage in a great deal of acting out, including violence toward parents and families. Disavowal, along with massive denial and projection, is used extensively. When intensive negative affects threaten to overwhelm the fragile psychic structure of these severely disturbed early adolescents, drugs and sex are used as a desperate attempt to avoid experiencing the pervasive loneliness, the sense of fragmentation, and the "black hole" that constantly lurks just beneath the surface.

Developmentally, early adolescents heavily involved with drugs appear to have a chronic lack of affect attunement and affect integration (Krystal, 1981, 1982, 1982/83; Socarides and Stolorow, 1984/85; Sugarman & Kurash, 1982).The parents, generally feeling quite empty themselves, foster the development of entitlement in the toddler. During early adolescence this entitlement and continued archaic grandiosity become intolerable for those around them. Their sense of entitlement is so strong, the battles over control so great, and the parents' feelings of weakness so intense, that outpatient psychotherapy is often not able to help the early adolescents and their families to provide the safety, structure, and consistency required to successfully limit the acting out. Unless this acting out can be contained, the underlying depression is not able to emerge and be worked through. When outpatient psychotherapy is not effective, hospitalization or residential placement is required.

SUMMARY

The development of a cohesive sense of self is dependent on the parents' ability to deal with the pain and the loss of giving up their ties with their early adolescents. These parental struggles include the pain of seeing their young teenagers developing other intense relationships and spending more time away from home. In addition, parents often have to learn to absorb and tolerate hostile comments from their young teenagers. All of these interactions are based, as stated by Kohut and Wolf (1978) not so much on what parents *do*, but who they *are* in determining whether they can maintain themselves as stable selfobjects for their early adolescents.

6

Treatment of the Early Adolescent

CASE EXAMPLE

The following case illustrates the chaotic nature and ensuing difficulties of working with young adolescents and their families in an outpatient setting. After one year of twice a week psychoanalytic psychotherapy, a 14-year-old male from a divorced family continued to fail classes, as well as have problems at home and with encopresis. The parents, both professionals, were involved in family sessions to help them, the mother in particular, to set limits, keep track of a weekly school report, and follow through with consequences. The mother continually berated the therapist and her ex-husband when she felt unjustly accused of "being the problem of her son not doing well."

Fortunately, the psychotherapist worked closely with this early adolescent's tutor who suddenly informed the psychotherapist of several events. First, the tutor reported that in spite of failing grades the patient continued to play baseball. Second, the mother scheduled her son to have ten teeth extracted three days before his finals started, which resulted in the patient's missing all of his finals. Last, the tutor stated that the mother approved a trip to Europe with the baseball team because she could not deprive her son of this "once in a life-time experience." She felt that the teachers would "understand" his not studying over spring break even though he was failing out of school.

An emergency meeting with the parents was called for the next day, a Saturday. The mother arrived fifteen minutes late with the announcement that the "family bird" was dead! Her "son had done it again—

he had forgotten to provide food and water for the bird!'' The father was also upset at this demonstrated continuation of the son's irresponsible behavior. What neither parent acknowledged was that the son had spent a week in bed at the father's house. The psychotherapist questioned the parents about why they had not been able to monitor the feeding of the bird, particularly the mother at whose house the bird stayed. The psychotherapist pointed out that while their son had assumed responsibility for the care of the bird, they as parents also had responsibility for overseeing the entire project. The parents were helped to see how they had not been able to facilitate their son's taking care of the pet as part of a maturing and positive experience. Instead, they had set up another shaming situation. Not only had they avoided seeing themselves as having any responsibility in the death of the bird, but they had not apologized for their role in the death of the bird. Once again, the son was at fault, in the same way as his not studying and not following through with his weekly report was "entirely" his responsibility. At this meeting, the parents were helped to see that they had to take responsibility with their son for problems that might arise and to become facilitators for their son.

At this same meeting, a decision was made for the son to live with his father and stepmother. Within several weeks, his grades improved from mainly F's to C's and B's. However, his problem with encopresis worsened as his greater involvement with school, including regular time for homework, stimulated being competitive and assertive. By his trying harder, he also became fearful of failing. Until now, this fear was so intense and frightening that he had defended against taking risks by stating: "I don't care!" and not doing well in school.

WHEN IS PSYCHOTHERAPY NECESSARY?

Traumatic life situations such as divorce, a loss of a significant family member, a change of school, job, home, or a serious physical illness creates stresses for individuals which they may or may not be able to handle. Traditionally, these life stresses have been seen as the traumatic event or catalyst that can derail the psychological development of an individual. Although young adolescents have been viewed as much more sensitive and vulnerable to these situational stresses because of the complex and profound changes they are experiencing, stress-related phenomena are often seen as precipitants of psychological distress in early adolescence.

While we believe traumatic life stresses often impede self-development, this chapter will attempt to show that psychopathology serious enough to bring young adolescents and their families into treatment is more often based on the innumerable microinjuries that are sustained during the first several years of life and which continue through childhood and adolescence. As discussed in previous chapters, these microinjuries result in a series of negative RIGs or FRIGs that leave a very fragile psychic structure. In addition, the entrance of early adolescents into formal operational thinking and the subsequent cognitive and emotional disequilibriums result in the further softening of this fragile psychic structure, which intensifies their struggles with lowered self-esteem and negative FRIGs.

The question remains: At what point do these difficulties necessitate early adolescents to seek psychotherapy? Our perspective suggests that it is the quality, or actually lack of quality, of the early adolescent–parental interactions, which facilitates the capacity to cope with these developmental issues. Obviously it is impossible to provide a constant affectively attuned environment for children. Developmentally, we have suggested a dual track which requires infants, children, and early adolescents to learn how to tolerate and sustain disappointments and frustrations, as well as good feelings and successes. This capacity to modulate feelings, at either pole, is often severely limited in families who do not appear to be able to weather the stresses of this phase of life. Signs of an inability to cope with situational stresses may be manifested by increased confusion, intense feelings of pressure, or anger toward parents, peers, or school authorities. Other signs of distress may include the onset of chaotic behavior, which may often be quite drastic and abrupt, particularly around confrontations at home over homework, friends, telephone privileges, and curfew times. Often parents become resentful of the friends their own young adolescents spend time with or bring home. These other teenagers, often much older and totally unfamiliar to the parents, may display aspects of poor self-esteem or show a lack of any goal-oriented direction. This new peer group may engage in frequent confrontations with authorities, including continual attacks on parents as part of their overall antiauthority and antischool attitude.

While there are no distinct or precise criteria that can serve as indicators of when psychotherapy is needed, parents usually have intense feelings of desperation, frustration, anger, or even rage about their relationship with their early adolescents. At these moments, everything seems to be unresolvable. This sense of absolute futility is often the catalyst for parents painfully acknowledging that their early adolescent, or more importantly the entire family, is in need of psychotherapy.

RESISTANCES TO PSYCHOTHERAPY

Initiating psychotherapy with early adolescents and their families is extremely difficult for the same reasons that make the early adolescent phase so unique, and yet so difficult. First, extensive cognitive changes foster an intense egocentrism which precipitates enormous fears of exposure and all the excruciating affects associated with shame. Hence, early adolescents often experience psychotherapy as walking into a "prison interrogation." This situation evokes images in young adolescents of an old grade-B movie—complete with the darkened room, the light shining in their face blinding them, and a faceless interrogator barking questions at them unmercifully. Early adolescents, knowing that their sentence has already been decided without a fair jury, await the verdict—imprisonment for life! At best, this mental image makes the commitment to psychotherapy terrifying for many, if not most, young teenagers.

Second, early adolescents have difficulties entering psychotherapy because of their extensive and pervasive use of disavowal and denial, which prevents them from experiencing or understanding their intense internal and interactional conflicts. In order to accept that they need psychotherapy, young adolescents have to acknowledge that a problem exists; to acknowledge a problem exists is to admit imperfection; to acknowledge imperfection is to admit that they are defective; being forced to admit that they are defective is to experience the terror of the "black hole." While this is a most intolerable and unacceptable state of mind for almost any individual, most young adolescents find this state of mind absolutely unacceptable at any cost! In other words, early adolescents have difficulties talking to a psychotherapist because it is too much like looking into a distorted mirror. They are afraid that once they look, the mirror will reflect and magnify even their slightest imperfections into enormous problems. They will resist and fight with all of their might for their inalienable right to be left alone. They want to believe that everything will be "fine!" In their own words, "It's

Okay!,'' ''It's over, don't worry about it.'' Because these early adolescents tend to be so heavily defended, they often do not experience the intensity or the painfulness of their various affect states. These distressing states of mind simply do not exist. With extensive use of disavowal and denial, affects are eliminated—banished from their psychic life. Consequently, young adolescents often do not have the motivation to relieve the psychic pain which psychotherapy provides as there is an almost total lack of awareness of this pain and the difficulties they are experiencing with their families, peers, or school.

THE PARENTAL ROLE

With the massive resistances of early adolescents to ''being exposed'' in psychotherapy, the role of parents becomes crucial in terms of presenting a ''united front'' when insisting that their young teenagers enter psychotherapy. Schimel (1974) has a comprehensive review of the importance of the two alliances in the treatment of adolescents that can be directly applied to working with early adolescents. Schimel describes the importance of developing a working alliance with the parents in addition to the therapeutic relationship with the adolescent. At the same time, providing a ''united front'' by the parents can be extremely difficult for parents, who themselves have to struggle with the arousal of feelings stemming from their own unresolved narcissistic injuries from this age period. These narcissistic injuries can include their realizing the ''defectiveness'' of their young teenagers as well as their own parenting skills. Oftentimes, when parents struggle to deal with their inadequacies as parents, they feel tremendously guilty about their inability to provide a safe, caring, and relatively unstressful environment for their youngsters. Unconscious issues about the use of their children to boost their own self-esteem will need to be worked through in their own psychotherapy. When parents are unable to face the reality of their problems and ''go along'' with the insistences of their early adolescents that ''everything is fine,'' they are reinforcing and perpetuating the pathological defense mechanisms of disavowal and denial and the concomitant family interactions that foster such pathological adaptations to the world.

While the sense of failure of parents for not being affectively or interactionally attuned to their early adolescents needs to be dealt with early in psychotherapy, families with borderline early adolescents must also address the issue of neurocognitive deficits. These neurocognitive deficits (Palombo, 1987) may prevent both early adolescents and parents from assimilating or processing information correctly. The end result is interactions that may not allow parents to be affectively attuned to their early adolescents, as well as early adolescents who are unable to take in the appropriate affect attunement of the parents in the manner in which it was intended.

When parents are unable to set limits to contain acting-out behavior, an outside agency, whether school, police, judicial system, or a child services agency, may need to confront the family's disavowal and denial of the seriousness of the problems. The outside agency's role may be to insist that psychotherapy be initiated. For example, a young Iranian junior high school student, who was referred to a mental health clinic by the local school psychotherapist, was removed from psychotherapy by her parents. There were several family dynamics that prevented this young female from receiving psychotherapy. In this case, the resistances of her parents were reinforced by a cultural attitude which viewed any form of psychotherapy as extremely shameful. Even a serious suicide attempt by this early adolescent was ignored by the family. When the local school authorities realized the extent and the seriousness of this young teenager's depression, they insisted that the parents become directly involved with treatment. However, the parents continued to minimize the difficulties and the extent of their daughter's problems. After the parents removed her from a psychiatric hospital, against medical advice, a child services agency was contacted because of the continued suicidal ideation of the youth. When the parents actually disappeared to avoid returning to psychotherapy, child abuse charges were filed. In order for this young teenage female to receive appropriate psychiatric treatment, she ultimately had to be rehospitalized by the police.

Clearly this dramatic example illustrates our point of the extreme difficulties of working with early adolescents and more importantly, their parents in psychodynamic psychotherapy. Often, parental issues arise that can result in the unfortunate avoidance and denial of the problems and need for psychotherapy of their early adolescents. Even within intact families, oftentimes one parent, usually the mother, wants the early adolescent to enter psychotherapy. However, if the other parent, whether consciously or unconsciously, is not supportive of the decision to seek help, their early adolescent senses this confusion or disagreement and is able to avoid entering treatment by "dividing and conquering'' the parents. This frequently occurs with unresolved marital issues which contaminate the parental alliance. While early adolescents from this type of family momentarily feel that they have ''won,'' they ultimately ''lose'' as they just become an unfortunate pawn in this ongoing battle between the parents.

Another type of problem arises when parents, often professionals, cannot deal with the shame and ensuing narcissistic injury that they experience when their children require the services of a mental health professional. Unconsciously, these parents often have a strong resistance to psychotherapy. In several cases, both authors were unsuccessful in trying to deal with the underlying shame and humiliation of the parents. For example, one author sensed a male early adolescent become increasingly resistent to psychotherapy. With each passage through the waiting room door, he experienced greater shame and humiliation. The psychotherapist attempted to discuss openly the patient's sense of shame and tried to meet with the parents to deal with their own ambivalences toward psychotherapy and their own sense of shame. In this one example, the family was unwilling to examine or deny any feelings of ambivalence or shame about the treatment. However, the mother felt increasingly powerless to bring her son in, while the father remained aloof and detached from the entire problem. Ultimately, with their son's increasing protests and daily tantrums the parents gave up and abruptly terminated treatment. One night, about a year later, the mother and son were seen on a street corner by the therapist who was parked across the street. The son was yelling at his mother as she frantically searched for money in her purse to buy a comic book. He continued to curse the mother as she became increasingly panicky, teary-eyed, and overwhelmed as she was unable to fulfill the incessant demands of her son. The psychotherapist, experiencing the shame, humiliation, and sense of helplessness of the mother, remained unseen.

The ability of early adolescents to ''divide and conquer'' is even more serious when the parents are openly battling one another. Frequently, early adolescents come into treatment because of the trauma of the divorce itself and the psychological distress of being caught in the middle of their divorced parents fighting over them—who has the early adolescent for the holidays, which parent should the early adolescent vacation with, and can the early adolescent wear clothing that the other parent bought. In these types of situations, bringing early adolescents into psychotherapy unfortunately becomes just another and all too convenient battle to wage in the parents' ongoing war. In this type of custody battle, early adolescents become slightly more than objects to fight over. The hostility of some of these parents is so intense that, more often than not, they cannot work through their anger at one another in order to understand empathetically how harmful this situation is for their early adolescents.

Even more intense resistance to psychotherapy arises when there is a bitter ongoing divorce or custody battle. Once again, early adolescents become trapped as pawns in the battle for control or revenge that often characterizes the unresolved issues between parents. These unresolved marital issues contaminate the ability of these parents to be affectively attuned to the needs of their early adolescents, and also create intense resistances to bringing their early adolescents and the families into psychotherapy.

Another type of resistance is from parents who do not feel that they have the "power" to bring their early adolescents into treatment. Often consciously, but more importantly unconsciously, these parents do not view themselves as competent adults. They do not have a firm sense of themselves as they continually struggle with negative self-esteem issues. Their poor sense of self-worth results in their believing that people will not listen or respect them. When these parents are confronted by their early adolescents, who believe that they can exist separate from the family, a serious obstacle to psychotherapy is created. Terrified by the implied or even direct threats of their early adolescents running away from home, these parents become paralyzed and accept their young teenager's way of thinking. In the parent's mind, taking a firm stand on their early adolescent's beginning psychotherapy might result in the imagined loss of their early adolescent and a further erosion of their parental identity. The resulting fear of total powerlessness by these parents makes commitment to psychotherapy for their early adolescents and families quite difficult, if not outright impossible.

Resolving this type of resistance can be accomplished only if the powerlessness and helplessness of the parents can be openly discussed and worked through. Working through this powerlessness allows these parents to gain better control of their severely acting-out early adolescents. Areas to work through include the triad of overidentification with the pain of their early adolescents, the parent's own sense of powerlessness, and their inability to set appropriate limits. This triad originally fostered and intensified the archaic grandiosity and sense of entitlement of their toddler and now returns in full force with their early adolescents. Parents who realize that they can gain some control over their early adolescents are able to work with the narcissistic injury of their young teenagers. Hopefully, this therapeutic work will eventually allow for a reunification of the family as a functioning unit and the capacity for greater self-differentiation for the adolescent.

On the other end of the spectrum are those early adolescents who are able to acknowledge to themselves and to their parents that they need help with self-esteem issues. These early adolescents tend to have difficulties dealing with their affects in three major areas. First, they have an inability to share affects with those close to them. They tend to hide their feelings, particularly negative ones. Second, they may have trouble attending school. Often, they are fearful and quite anxious, especially at the beginning of a new school year or every Sunday evening. These early adolescents have frequent stomachaches or headaches and they make multiple phone calls from school asking to be taken home. Last, these early adolescents often seem to have considerable fears and difficulties at night because of problems dealing with their negative affects, especially anger.

These sleep problems have two components. First, there is a difficulty falling asleep. This may be related to their minds steadily racing about their problems with their friends, with school, and with their lives. They constantly go over homework or events trying to find the "right" or "perfect" solution. Falling asleep often appears to involve a sense of losing control over what is frightening. In addition, they have very vivid and active imaginations, which, when coupled with their difficulties with anger, results in shadows and noises becoming creatures, monsters, and burglars coming to "get them." Also, these early adolescents are afraid that once they do fall asleep they will awaken because of a terrifying dream, which may be precipitated by a sense of self-fragmentation or a fear of psychic disintegration. These terrifying realities often require parents to be physically present either in the teenager's or parents' bedroom.

In general, these parents are able to engage in psychotherapy with their early adolescents. They will take an active role in understanding their contribution to the difficulties of their young teenagers. Usually, these parents have better self-esteem and self-worth than the other parents we have discussed. When reflecting on their own adolescence, they seem to have fewer and less intense issues centering around shame and humiliation. As a consequence, they have less of a need to use disavowal and denial on a massive level. They are more easily motivated to understand their own unresolved conflicts and the role these unresolved conflicts have played in the difficulties of their early adolescents. This capacity of parents greatly assists the improvement of the family situation. In particular, the parents can become more effective in facilitating affect integration and providing a more supportive environment to strengthen their adaptive capabilities. These changes, in turn, assist early adolescents with their self-esteem.

QUALITIES OF AN EARLY ADOLESCENT PSYCHOTHERAPIST

Even when the stage seems to be set for psychotherapy, there are still difficulties, including the critical choice of a therapist. Young adolescents may accept the inevitability of seeing a psychotherapist and parents are determined to do whatever they need to bring their children into the therapist's office. However, there is still the issue of finding a psychotherapist who works well with early adolescents and their families.

We believe that a psychotherapist who works with young teenagers and their families must first and foremost have the ability to be empathetically and affectively attentive, not only to the early adolescent, but to the entire family. Papoušek and Papoušek (1983) comment about "intuitive parenting," which has relevance to working with early adolescents. They believe that trying to analyze and understand the parenting process may adversely effect the natural and spontaneous interactions between infants and parents. We too believe that this concept has relevance for work with early adolescents. There are times when trying to be "too intellectual," or "too analytical" can interfere with the affective interaction that plays an important part in our work, the repair of misattunements between parents and early adolescents.

Psychotherapists should also be able to accept the need of young adolescents for a sense of safety and protection. Additionally, a clinician needs to be aware of the conscious and unconscious fears that these patients have in terms of opening up the "black hole," a metaphor easily understood and used by this age group to describe their severe depression. Hunger for attention is related to long histories of severe disappointments revolving around rejections by parents who are too limited emotionally and physically to be available. Early adolescents need to feel that their psychotherapist is available and attuned to their needs and feelings.

Unfortunately, the term "empathic" has become a misnomer in many ways. During consultations at various institutions, one of the authors has experienced psychotherapists working with this age group who believe that being nice is being empathic. Being nice is not the same as providing a safe, nurturing environment for early adolescents with a Narcissistic Personality Disorder. Being nice is particularly destructive when used with acting-out early adolescents. For early adolescents with as Narcissistic Behavior Disorder, being nice is the opposite of being empathic. Only firm limits, constant confrontations of their acting out and their use of disavowal will help these seriously disturbed patients. Only in an environment in which they feel contained and safe enough to allow all the negative and overwhelming affects and fears to surface will they be able to work through issues centering around their depression (Holtzman, 1982/83). Psychotherapists who hunger for acceptance and who are unable or unwilling to set appropriate limits to confront the acting out of their patients are not being empathic. Being empathic implies an understanding of the issues and an ability to deal with these issues with compassion and firmness.

WORKING WITH EARLY ADOLESCENTS

The remainder of this chapter describes the treatment of early adolescents. Esman (1985) is one psychotherapist who acknowledges and accepts the unique struggles, difficulties, and fears of this age group. Because this age group is often unresponsive to conventional psychoanalytic interpretations, he does not appear to "force" interpretations. Esman appears to be quite content to "be there" for early adolescents without demanding compliance to his own personal "agenda." The idea of just accepting early adolescents can be explained with an example. Oftentimes when a psychotherapist first begins to work with early adolescent patients, they may ask for food or bring their own food into the session. Hopefully, they are not immediately "fed" an interpretation by the psychotherapist as well. Rather than explaining to early adolescents the hidden or underlying dynamics of why they are hungry, it often appears more effective to foster an alliance with these patients by first responding to their hunger, including feeding them if the psychotherapist can feel comfortable doing this.

DIAGNOSTIC CATEGORIES OF EARLY ADOLESCENT PSYCHOPATHOLOGY

To formulate an appropriate and effective treatment program for early adolescents, a tentative or working hypothesis that explains the behavioral difficulties, interactional problems, and psychic struggles of each early adolescent is critical. Three diagnostic options or classifications will be discussed: Neurotic Disorders, Narcissistic Personality Disorders, and Narcissistic Behavior Disorders, which includes the category of the borderline early adolescent. Suggestions on how to deal with these various categories of patients are discussed.

Neurotic Disorders of Early Adolescence

Although we believe pure "neurotic" disorders of early adolescence or disorders based on Oedipal conflict are currently quite rare, this diagnostic possibility must still be considered. The psychic structure of neurotic youths are "intact." This, in essence, means that their parents were "good enough." With these early adolescents, parents do not require their children to serve as selfobjects for their own needs, particularly in infancy or early childhood. Only later, during the oedipal period when these parents may require their children to serve more as a sexual object do problems begin. The problem even at this age is mainly internalized conflicts. The predominance of the internal nature of this conflict continues into early adolescence. Young teenagers with a Neurotic Disorder might manifest certain symptoms, such as, depression, school phobias, obsessions, anxiety states, and encopresis.

Narcissistic Disorders of Early Adolescence

In comparison to neurotic early adolescents, early adolescents with narcissistic or borderline pathological disorders have experienced greater deficits in parenting, with their parents not being "good enough" enough of the time. Deficits in parenting can come from a variety of sources. These parents may not be able to handle parenthood because of their own psychological problems; the parents may be struggling with narcissistic or borderline issues themselves. Another possibility is that parents with a healthier psychic structure may be struggling with the death of a significant other or experiencing a major depression. As a result parents have a limited capacity to parent at that moment. Additionally, inadequate parenting skills can be related to a parent's immaturity, external situational pressures, or just plain indifference. These types of situations create an emotionally empty environment for children who, as they enter early adolescence experience an internal emptiness. These early adolescents have psychopathology based more on interpersonal problems rather than the almost exclusively intrapsychic conflicts of neurotic early adolescents. Their fragile self-esteem and lack of a set of solid organizing principles leaves these early adolescents vulnerable to the availability of external support systems.

In these problematic family situations, children are required to meet the selfobject needs of the parents rather than the parents being available for the selfobject needs of their children. Because of these types of interactions, children suffer early and severe depressions, which prevent the formation of a true sense of self.

There are two types of narcissistic problems that develop from these pathological interactions based on the concepts postulated by Kohut (1971, 1977, 1984) and Kohut and Wolf (1978). The first category includes early adolescents with a Narcissistic Personality Disorder. This is the healthier and more treatable of the two categories of narcissistic disorders. The second category, Narcissistic Behavior Disorder, includes early adolescents who have more intense struggles with self-cohesion and self-esteem. These struggles are the result of earlier and more intense microinjuries from chronic selfobject failures from their parents and caregivers. This category blends with the diagnostic category of borderline early adolescents. In both of these diagnostic categories, parents have not been available to function as appropriate selfobjects. Palombo (1987), writing about borderline children presents an argument that all borderline children, and we would assume all borderline early adolescents, have a neurocognitive impairment as may many of their parents. These neurocognitive deficits contribute significantly to the inability of the dyad to feel understood and attuned to each other.

Narcissistic Personality Disorder of Early Adolescence

Within the diagnostic category Narcissistic Personality Disorder, the psychic structure of the parents is more intact when compared with the parents whose children have Narcissistic Behavior Disorder problems. These parents have less of a need to use their children as selfobjects and often have their own fears and an intense sense of helplessness when dealing with the world. These parents transmit à la Stern's (1985) template a similar if not more intense fear of the world onto their children. The way in which they interact with their children sets up certain RIGs and FRIGs which persist throughout childhood. These parents have their own fears of aggression as well as struggles with their children expressing anger. Their children, particularly when they are extremely bright, sensitive, and perceptive, sense and learn that their parents are unable to deal with the world (Burch, 1985).

Parents of early adolescents with Narcissistic Personality Disorders also have difficulties allowing their children to separate and individuate. When these youngsters enter early adolescence, they become increasingly fearful and inhibited. They are often extremely bright but have problems at school, particularly around competitive issues. These young teenagers may become school phobic when they enter junior high school. They also have trouble with situations away from home including overnight camp or sleeping over at a friend's house.

Parental fears and anxieties set up the earliest RIGs for these early adolescents. For example, one parent feared, from the day she knew she was pregnant, that one day her son would be taken away from her. Unbeknown to her, her early adolescent son also grew up with a fear of being kidnapped in the middle of the night by two men. These parallel fantasies actually became a reality when the young adolescent required placement at a long-term treatment facility. One afternoon, the son was awakened from a nap by two attendants who took him to a mental health facility. While the son was soon able to appreciate his parents actions in protecting him, the son's hospitalization was more traumatic for the mother than if he had been kidnapped.

Early adolescents with Narcissistic Personality Disorders have difficulties experiencing their anger, as well as expressing their anger. As stated before, they have difficulties falling asleep because they "can't stop thinking!" Many are also extremely fearful of falling asleep either because they are terrified of losing control or because of their constant fear of being awakened in the middle of the night by a nightmare. Their fears of a catastrophe occurring are so fragmenting to their sense of intactness that they require the presence of their parents to fall asleep. Many times they are so terrified that they are unable to go back to sleep in their own bedroom, even with a parent. Instead, they require the constant presence of parents to protect them, to help them modulate and control their overwhelming feelings and fears. Often these early adolescents end up sleeping on the floor in their parents' bedroom.

Gradually, the parents begin to feel suffocated and become enraged at their early adolescents and experience their early adolescents as being extremely babyish and absolutely inconsiderate. The parents themselves are fearful and they are unable to express their anger or anxiety about setting limits. Their hesitation serves to intensify the fears of their early adolescents who sense the anger and difficulties their parents have dealing with these affects. One consequence of such interactions is that early adolescents become even more terrified of being left alone in the middle of the night and of the world in general.

These early adolescents are faced with intense psychic conflicts that require a combination of individual psychotherapy as well as family therapy. Parental participation can be in the form of either family therapy, conjoint therapy, or individual psychotherapy. The adjunctive treatment will depend on the psychological strengths of the parents and their own support systems. Parents are helped to understand the process of psychotherapy with their early adolescents as well as the family systems. However, whenever early adolescents are viewed as the "identified patient" by the parents, as the one to be "fixed," treatment is less effective and proceeds more slowly until this viewpoint is worked through and altered.

Narcissistic Behavior Disorders of Early Adolescence

Early adolescents with a Narcissistic Behavior Disorder and their families are even more difficult to work with because they use and maintain a greater degree of disavowal and denial. In fact, they are so heavily defended that they often do not experience their psychic discomfort, in spite of severe problems at home, school, and with peers. Parents of these children have more severe emotional struggles themselves. Most likely, these parents have required their children, since infancy, to function as selfobjects more extensively than the parents of early adolescents with a Neurotic or Narcissistic Personality Disorder. These parents have unconscious needs for their children to take care of them.

This has been graphically and poignantly described by A. Miller (1981) in her book *Prisoners of Childhood: The Drama of the Gifted Child and the Search for the True Self* as well as in her subsequent writings (1983, 1984). The lack of "good enough" parenting early in life leaves these early adolescents in a state of internal chaos. Without a sense of soothing RIGs (Stern, 1985) or patterns of things getting better (Demos, 1982, 1983, 1984; Demos and Kaplan, 1986) these early adolescents are quite susceptible to becoming overwhelmed by the severe and incapacitating depression that lurks just below the surface. To avoid being overwhelmed by the "black hole," they withdraw into the culture of drugs, sex, and peers who only want fun now—no future and no past (Krystal, 1982; Sugarman and Kurash, 1982).

Psychotherapy with these early adolescents is extremely difficult. Their depression is so totally warded off by disavowal, denial, and projection that they experience only intense anger fostered by chronic misattunements. This anger and their suspiciousness of getting close to anyone makes them extremely resistant to any form of help. Their parents, who recall their own intensified fears of the world and sense of helplessness, are at times unable to take a firm stand and insist that their early adolescents seek out treatment.

Rage permeates the psychic life of these extremely disturbed adolescents and their families. They are ready for revenge and they retaliate with a vengeance, an "eye for an eye." This rage often makes family sessions major battle grounds. When parents do participate in family therapy, their own fears and narcissistic vulnerabilities make it extremely difficult for them to tolerate the intensity of these sessions. Because these families are so vulnerable and fragile, the authors will often see these patients separately in order to protect them from the unleashed anger of their early adolescents and to prevent further destruction of the family ties.

In these situations, early adolescents are seen individually to try to establish a safe place for them to allow their depression and angry feelings to surface slowly. However, unlike early adolescents with a Narcissistic Personality Disorder, these early adolescents need firmer limits and structure, even in psychotherapy.

Basch discusses the use of confrontation with patients displaying disavowal by stating that the analyst must "listen carefully for what the patient leaves out, glosses over, mentions only in passing, treats as trivial, and so on. The resolution of disavowal involves the analyst in active questioning, exploration of inconsistencies, and possible confrontation of the patient with the significance of his nonverbal or minimally verbal behavior. It necessitates not only the analyst's activity

but at times may place him in the position of challenging the patient''
(Basch, 1985, p. 39).

Psychotherapy should focus on helping to set safe and firm limits for
the family because these early adolescents require greater structure to
make up for their lack of internal consistency, that is, organizing principles and psychic structure. Sessions with parents will need to focus
on: (1) the self-esteem problems of the parents; (2) the unresolved issues
of the parents' own adolescence that they may be struggling with; (3)
parenting issues relating to the establishment of firmer and more appropriate limits, and (4) ways parents can become more affectively
attuned to the needs of their early adolescents.

The issue of setting limits is extremely important as these parents
have probably projected a sense of helplessness onto their early adolescents since infancy and have tried unsuccessfully since then to shelter
them from the world. As discussed earlier, this triad of overidentification
with the pain of their children, the sense of helplessness of the parents,
and the inability to set appropriate limits due to the unconscious wish
for their children to be stronger and more forceful in dealing with the
world, sets up the pattern for the intensification of the archaic grandiosity
and sense of entitlement. These children never develop RIGs or FRIGs
with which they can successfully learn to experience and cope with
frustration, boredom, and pain.

With any situation or event that activates these feelings which become
intolerable, these parents, if their early adolescents are to remain at
home, must learn to set limits to help provide a contained and protected
environment. However, these parents often have the greatest difficulty
saying ''no'' to provide appropriate limits. Yet paradoxically, these
parents are, at the same time, the parents that must take the firmest
stands with their early adolescents. They must also be rigidly consistent
if they hope to keep their early adolescents at home. When the family
systems, as well as these early adolescents, are not able to change, or
not change fast enough for the safety and well-being of the early adolescents and family, residential, or hospital placement may be required.

THERAPEUTIC STRATEGIES

Our therapeutic approach for once or twice a week psychodynamically
oriented psychotherapy focuses on self-development and the repair of

the selfobject ties, with a primary emphasis on the interaction between the early adolescent patient and therapist. Successful mirroring and idealizing interactions are crucial. While the authors do not discount sexual and aggressive issues, the uncovering and interpretations of resistances to these drives are not as critical as helping these early adolescents to feel safe and understood. Treatment goals and approaches must be individualized and customized to each patient. Basically, there are no definitive rules. However, there are several treatment interventions which we believe are crucial when working with early adolescent patients.

Classical psychoanalytic writers, who work with early adolescents, have tended to transfer the psychoanalytic stance and technique of silence and interpretation used with their adult patients to their work with early adolescents with as few modifications as possible. Our approach, based on our theoretical understandings, is more animated and active. Our approach also uses the concept of optimal responsiveness (Bacal, 1985) as defined in Chapter 4, as well as the fostering of the dual developmental tract for both positive and negative affects (Demos and Kaplan, 1986; Beebe and Lachmann, 1988).

Silence

First, the minimal use of silence is often critical when working with most early adolescents, especially when psychotherapy is limited to once or twice a week. We believe silences are experienced in a number of ways by early adolescents. Most often, silences are experienced as misattunements as these early adolescents have already experienced multiple misattunements or the lack of appropriate selfobject functions by their parents. These faulty interactions have left early adolescents with a lack of soothing RIGs and FRIGs and, hence, they lack a consistent set of organizing principles and lack psychic structure. The persistent use of silence often perpetuates these traumas. Silences can also be experienced as depriving, as hostile, and as a way of engaging in a passive-aggressive power struggle, which recreates the pathological interactions within their own families. In summary, as stated by Kohut (1987), silences are not neutral. These same silences can also be experienced as quite shameful and humiliating.

The issue of silence does not mean that there should be an outright avoidance of silence. The therapist must consider the emotional and cognitive level of functioning of their patients to determine what the experience of silence or lack of silence means to these patients. For example, early adolescents who are still functioning at the concrete operational thinking level of a grammar school youngster, especially when needing to disavow or deny affects and problems, will rarely be able to tolerate or comprehend silence as helpful or empathic, even when the psychotherapist may believe that this will allow the unfolding of unconscious material. Often early adolescents have experienced silence as a weapon either used against them, or as a weapon that they have used against their parents. Silence, unfortunately, in the context of the therapist's office often recreates this pathological and destructive interaction.

Free Association or Structured Sessions?

The concept of free association is a valuable and essential tool of psychoanalytic psychotherapy with adults. However, due to the chaotic state of mind of most early adolescents, they often require structure in their daily life, including at times, structured psychotherapy sessions. By a structured session, we mean that the psychotherapist picks up cues of an important theme early in the session and encourages the discussion of this topic through questions, encouragement, and on occasions some silences to further develop this theme. This approach may include guiding the discussion and even returning over and over again to a topic, particularly when there is a strong avoidance of a vital and important issue that is causing problems at home or at school. This also requires the psychotherapist to know when to back off, when further exploration will only result in the patient experiencing the session as an interrogation. Thus, questions concerning a fight with parents, poor grades, or a loss of a friend will frequently be met with resistance, usually silence, and occasionally anger.

For many early adolescents, talking about anything other than in monosyllabic exchanges is too much. Playing cards or other activities, used for years quite readily by psychotherapists working with latency children, are then used, oftentimes exclusively except during family sessions. Regular contact with parents is necessary, even if by phone, to provide details of what is occurring at home, at school, and with peers. Parents are told to assume that the psychotherapist will know nothing of what is happening in the daily life of their early adolescent unless parents routinely contact him/her.

Cognitive Functioning

The cognitive functioning of early adolescents is another critical issue in determining a therapeutic approach in working with early adolescents. While some level of formal operational thinking is already available, especially in very intelligent and creative teenagers, psychotherapists cannot assume that early adolescents can always use their logical thinking to just "stay with the facts!" When young teenagers are confronted with emotional issues, they have great difficulties looking at all alternatives objectively and dealing with their own inconsistencies, faults, or defects. In other words, early adolescents may be able to discuss complicated science projects or philosophical issues, but when they are asked to look at or discuss areas that arouse considerable conflicts and affects, they suddenly seem back in the world of concrete operational children. This inability to think logically or remain objective becomes even more impossible when the affects are intense, particularly over shame and anger. These affects perpetuate or reactivate the defense mechanisms of disavowal, denial, and projection, which create a fixation or regression in cognitive capacities which makes working with early adolescents, particularly in a logical manner, quite difficult.

There are always exceptions, even to this generalization. One male early adolescent from a very concrete thinking family amazed the psychotherapist by his ability to tolerate not only silence but his ability to discuss his dreams on a regular basis. The dreams had numerous themes of intense conflicts with his younger brother, as well as with his father. He was totally fascinated by his dreams and our discussions of them, even though the dreams were emotionally quite intense. Unfortunately, the parents had difficulty with their son seeing a psychiatrist and they abruptly terminated treatment. The parents stated that their son had to learn to "sink or swim," as they felt that he could not spend his entire life seeing a psychotherapist.

Interacting with Early Adolescents

How does one deal with early adolescents? Most importantly, we feel that psychotherapists must be able to understand and respect their vulnerabilities.

The capacity to accept the concrete thinking of early adolescents under stress is crucial. The affective interactions between patients and psychotherapists is basic to developing psychological insight and psychological growth. The therapeutic relationship should be based on caring, valuing the needs and vulnerabilities of these early adolescents, and setting appropriate limits when necessary. When this style of interaction is successful, the patient will have a new experience with the psychotherapist. Hopefully this experience will be more positive then those experienced previously so that new FRIGs can be created.

From the parents' perspective, psychotherapists are fortunate as they do not have to live with their patients twenty-four hours a day. Psychotherapists start "clean and fresh" as they do not have the years of struggles, conflicts, and intense encounters that have worn the family down. Hopefully, when a strong, positive connection is made during the first several sessions, the excitement and the "gleam in the therapist's eye" will be apparent to the early adolescent patients. The interactions with the psychotherapist will often be in sharp contrast to their continued struggles with their parents.

One specific issue which seems to reappear in the treatment of early adolescents with Neurotic or Narcissistic Personality Disorders is an inability to deal with various affects, particularly aggression. These patients are terrified of asserting themselves because of unresolved aggressive conflicts. Because of this struggle with unresolved aggressive issues, they are unable to deal with their competitive feelings. Our strategy for developing competitiveness, when talking is not effective, is to involve early adolescents in games.

Early adolescents, with their fears of interrogation and having someone read their minds, often end up with intense feelings of helplessness and shame which preclude them from wanting to talk about anything. Although many therapists will readily bring out a game to engage a latency child, they are reluctant to do so with early adolescents. However, for the authors, a more important issue than cognitive understanding is the affective interaction—the relationship between patient and psychotherapist. The relationship, based on caring, the valuing of the vulnerabilities and needs of the early adolescents, and appropriate limit setting, creates new FRIGs. By this we mean that there is a new experience with a new ending. These early adolescent patients experience the excitement, "the gleam in the eye" from their psychotherapist.

One fourteen-year-old boy was seen for one and one-half years after his parents brought him into treatment following a sports accident, which left this former "golden boy" struggling with school, friends, and even with his family. This young adolescent totally refused to discuss anything that was troubling him. Actually, he always felt that everything was "fine" because of his intense struggle with self-esteem issues and his overwhelming fear of being exposed, shamed, and humiliated. This patient at first found double solitaire quite frightening. During the second year of treatment, he became increasingly competitive, assertive, and emotionally demonstrative in his play with the psychotherapist. This work was combined with regular (one to two per month) family meetings or meetings with only his parents to help them deal with his various problems as well as those related to their parenting issues. The change in this early adolescent, especially with his peers and school, was directly related to the increased confidence, assertiveness, and competitiveness shown in his card playing. Several years later this male returned during his senior year of high school to deal openly with his struggles with self-esteem that he was unable to do several years before. His openness in focusing on his fears and struggles with self-esteem issues helped him in his adjustment to moving away from home to college. Even more importantly, at college he was able to eventually choose a profession that was his childhood dream, becoming an Air Force pilot, a profession his parents, particularly his mother, had always actively discouraged.

A similar approach was also used with a twelve-year-old male who required a brief hospitalization. There was no talking between the patient and the psychotherapist either in the first several months in the office or during his psychiatric hospitalization. His comments to anything were always, "Fine!" This young adolescent had no capacity to listen to anything I said, let alone listen or respond to any "interpretations." Yet, over a period of two and one-half years, which included seven months in the hospital with conjoint sessions with the parents and family meetings as we approached termination in the hospital, the patient demonstrated drastic changes in his play and more importantly in his interactions with parents, family, and psychotherapist. At the end of psychotherapy, the then fifteen-year-old was functioning in a gifted program. He had made new friends and he was also a totally different person at home. While he was talkative at the end of psychotherapy and could even laugh and play with the psychotherapist, any attempt to try to reconstruct the events leading up to the psychiatric hospitalization, the hospitalization itself, and the changes that he had made during psychotherapy were met with massive and total resistance.

Working with this age group is extremely difficult as oftentimes there is no "one way" to engage them. While playing games can be one approach, psychotherapists, must be careful not to become bogged down in games, which early adolescents very conveniently use to prevent "looking in the mirror." Yet, the authors have had early adolescents do both games and talking, as well as going out for snacks, playing darts, asking the psychotherapist for help with their homework, and even conducting "scientific experiments." This latter approach occurred with one early adolescent who had requested to see a psychotherapist because of an inability to sleep alone, regularly occurring nightmares, and frequent headaches. Besides occasional double solitaire, these sessions were at first spent trying to figure out his headache patterns. We discovered a correlation with headaches on days of tests, major papers, and verbal reports. The headaches, nightmares, problems sleeping alone, and his school work problems all improved in parallel with his developing an improved sense of self-esteem and a greater ability to be assertive, competitive, and emotionally more expressive, much of this worked through in our weekly double solitaire games.

Some patients, particularly several girls in treatment with both psychotherapists, spent months sitting in our offices totally silent. In these cases, the parents were brought into the twice weekly psychotherapy sessions. The parents became an integral part of psychotherapy by discussing the anger of their daughters and their reactions in the presence of their stubbornly silent early adolescents. Invariably, the silence in the office immediately changed to rage toward the parents on the way home for forcing them to attend psychotherapy. The parents were educated and "coached" by being encouraged to look at their own struggles with anger, how they had difficulties dealing with anger with their daughters, and how they needed to "allow" their daughters to be angry, toward both the psychotherapist and their parents. There was a parallel process in which the authors helped the parents tolerate intense affects, in this case anger and rage, with the parents. The parents then helped their daughters to tolerate their own intense feelings of anger and rage. The parents were also helped to set appropriate limits as well as to understand the reasons and needs of their early adolescents to "survive" their own anger.

In one case, the parents, through their effective parenting alliance

(Cohen and Weissman, 1984) were able to support each other in accepting and enduring their daughter's frustration, pain, and anger. Surviving the daughter's silence was essential in helping their daughter go through this very "frustrating and boring" psychotherapy. Her fear of the dark, her inability to sleep in her own bedroom, and her phobic tendencies at school, especially with the entrance into junior high after a move to a different city, were all overcome with the increased ability of the parents and later the daughter to tolerate the various feelings of frustration, pain, anger, and boredom through the family's work in the therapist's office and individual sessions.

In a similar situation in which the parents were in the midst of a divorce and could not provide the parenting alliance (Cohen and Weissmann, 1984), the outcome was not successful. The female early adolescent refused to continue psychotherapy and she engaged in a power struggle in the office by using silence. With no support or encouragement from the father, the family soon faded out of therapy as the daughter refused to come to the psychotherapist's office, and the mother, unable to separate herself from her daughter and overidentified with the daughter's pain, did not feel she could force an intolerable situation on her daughter. The psychotherapist experienced the ambivalence of the 13-year-old female in the office. There were times when she talked openly and times when she was upset and refused to speak. The other psychotherapist also saw the patient several times running up the steps with a big smile on her face, seemingly looking forward to the session. The grandiosity, the omnipotence, which covered over the tremendous fears and insecurities of the young adolescent were never confronted, explored, and worked through as the mother decided that psychotherapy was "not right for her daughter at this time." The parents continued their embittered divorce struggle and the daughter continued to remain enmeshed with her mother, both desperately trying to protect the other from the very frightening outside world.

SUMMARY

Working with early adolescents is exciting, challenging, and at times frustrating. This age group uses primitive defense mechanisms, including disavowal, massive denial, and projection to defend against shame, the core affect of early adolescence. In this chapter, the importance of working with parents and families is emphasized, as the role of parents is crucial in having early adolescents begin psychotherapy. Treatment issues as well as therapeutic strategies are described.

7

Adolescence Proper: The Consolidation of Psychic Structure

THE TRANSITION INTO ADOLESCENCE PROPER

Our contemporary society's social and cultural "rite of passage" into adolescence proper is symbolized by the obtainment of a driver's license, generally at sixteen years of age. Inherent in this recognition is the expectation of more adult-like behaviors by youngsters, who previously were viewed as immature and more dependent on adults for support and guidance. Unlike the specific date for a driver's license, psychological signs of movement into adolescence proper are often less tangible and, in many ways, are recognized only in hindsight.

One such example is a conversation heard at a recent meeting of eleventh grade parents at a local high school:

All during grammar school, my daughter would say good-bye to me in the morning as she left for school. Then when she started junior high, it began. I never heard her say good-bye to me again for the next three years. When she finally did say 'Good-bye Mom, see you later,' she was almost sixteen years old. It was such a relief to be treated as if I was once again worth acknowledging. At the same time, I could not believe that her self-centeredness might be diminishing. She actually wanted to talk to me. She wanted me to meet her friends, to go shopping with her, to see her new clothes. I didn't feel like I needed to hide in the trunk of the car when I had to take her somewhere. I no longer felt like a leper. She even knew that I existed for reasons other than to drive her somewhere, buy her clothes, or be available to feed her and her friends. I sensed that I had gotten through her early adolescence when she said:

'Mom, you look so tired, I bet that you had a really hard day!' I felt like crying, it was such a relief to realize that once more I mattered to her.

Parents, teachers, siblings, and even adolescents themselves as they enter high school years suddenly realize that their lives are different. Life is calmer for everyone involved. The "roller coaster" or "yo-yo" nature of early adolescence begins to subside. Although there is no one event or action that seems to signify the end of this unique developmental phase, young teenagers, who were intensively emotional and erratic only a short time before, are now capable of looking at themselves and reflecting on possible actions before they react. With a greater sense of cause and effect and a desire to be a participant in a larger social system, adolescents are no longer experienced by those around them as "the center of the universe." Adolescents can now recognize and accept themselves as a satellite, as part of the solar system. Once again, they are a member of their family.

Crucial to this transition from early adolescence to adolescence proper is a consolidation or solidifying of their psychic structure. The consolidation of their psychic structure at a higher level of cognitive functioning results in a greater reliance on internal support for the maintenance of their set of organizing principles.

Not all adolescents, however, function at a level of formal operational thinking. In fact, many adolescents never fully attain formal operational thinking, but rather consolidate their cognitive capacity at a concrete operational level of thinking, with varying aspects of formal operational thinking integrated into their cognitive structure. Whenever this lower level of thinking predominates, the psychic rigidity experienced in early adolescence remains as these adolescents, or even adults, continue to be dependent on more primitive defense mechanisms. Disavowal, denial, and projection persist. Adolescents, however, who are in a family and school environment which encourages abstract thinking, are able to attain the consolidation of varying degrees of formal operational thinking. Functioning at a higher cognitive level provides adolescents with a system of thinking that is less vulnerable to external trauma as well as less dependent on external support from their selfobjects. The strengthening of the capacity to use formal operational thinking in adolescence proper is based upon the repeated successes of early adolescents in dealing with everyday situations and stressful life events on an abstract level. These repeated successes allow for the development of a new set of FRIGs that give adolescents a sense that they can master increasingly more complex situations, including the affects aroused, no matter how intense.

In other words, the extent to which mastery of early adolescence is attained depends on the strength of their set of organizing principles, or psychic structure. As during earlier phases, early adolescents, who have a more confident sense about themselves, enter adolescence proper with a greater sense of mastery toward their world. This sense of mastery allows for a firmer psychic foundation and a diminished need for external support systems to maintain their psychic equilibrium. On the other hand, early adolescents who have poor self-esteem and poor self-esteem regulation due to chronic selfobject misattunements, enter adolescence proper with a faulty or incomplete sense of mastery and a pseudo-foundation toward their world. These adolescents are more vulnerable to the "black hole" (Grotstein, 1987)—the empty depression or sense of self-fragmentation experienced with stressful events.

On the whole, adolescents with a more positive sense of self-esteem and a healthier self-esteem regulation can deal more effectively with stressful and emotionally laden issues. Greenspan (1979), a pioneer in the integration of cognitive abilities and affects along a drive-theory model, describes the higher level of functioning or "closed system" of adolescents who have obtained formal operational thinking. These adolescents are capable of dealing with intense affects and stressful situations in a self-contained manner. In this concept of a self-contained or closed system, adolescents are able to take in (assimilate) a vast range of different stimuli (variables) without the structure having to modify itself (accommodate) in any way. As these adolescents are capable of using more mature defense mechanisms, they have a greater ability for increased self-reflection and introspection. While only a short time before certain topics would have resulted in avoidance at any cost, these more reflective and insightful states of mind allow adolescents to deal with more emotionally charged thoughts and feelings such as death and dying, mortality, and sexuality. This increased ability to deal with such emotionally charged issues in a more thoughtful and intellectual manner fosters the exploring of affects, even intense ones, without losing contact with their own emotional and unconscious lives. These adolescents are able to experience ideas, wishes and feelings simultaneously in thought. This provides a greatly enhanced freedom and psychic mobility, a calmness that was not previously available. This increased calmness also extends to relationships with family and friends. This is a distinct difference from early adolescents, adolescents who remain in concrete operational thinking, or even many adults who must continue to use disavowal, denial, and projection to deal with overwhelming situations and the ensuing arousal of affects.

An example of this distinction can be seen in the reaction by adolescents to doing poorly on a test. Early adolescents often hide the "D" or "F" from themselves as well as from their parents. This hiding or obliterating their poor performance does not allow them to understand their role in the problem. This mode of hiding also does not allow early adolescents to ask for help, particularly relevant in relationship to their parents. Asking parents for help, especially by adolescents who are already insecure and vulnerable, activates intense feelings of being overwhelmed and shamed. In contrast, healthier adolescents, who do not need to blame teachers for putting material on the test that was not covered in class, look at their own role in their poor performance. In addition, they seek out alternatives to correct the problem, which may even include asking their parents for help. Adolescents can use their disappointment or shame of doing poorly to help motivate them to study harder. They also experience the test as only a single event in their lives, rather than an all-or-nothing test of their competency and sense of self-worth.

In summary, this consolidation of formal operational thinking during this phase has three significant consequences. First, adolescents return to a more internal means of support in their psychic lives. This internal support frees adolescents from the intense fragility and subsequent ambivalent dependence on selfobject ties. With a sense of a firmer psychic foundation, due to both the consolidation of cognitive development and the lessening of the physical, pubertal and social pressures, the cognitive and emotional disequilibriums of early adolescence begin to fade. The chaotic nature of their lives, the extreme narcissistic vulnerability, the intense egocentrism, and the all too frequent overwhelming sense of shame all begin to dissipate as powerful intruders into their emotional life. With their calmer states of mind, adolescents are less compelled to massively shut out whole parts of their psychic lives.

Second, the maturation of their psychic structure, through the consolidation of their cognitive thinking, leads to a lessening of their egocentrism, or a "decentering" (Looft, 1971). This lessening of their egocentrism results in adolescents not having to be as concerned about being caught or being shamed in front of the "imaginary audience." This ensuing sense of feeling more intact provides adolescents with a firmer psychic foundation to reflect upon situations, issues, and struggles and allows adolescents to take greater risks. They feel more comfortable "playing" with their ideas and of experiencing their ideas and related affect states, even in front of a class full of peers.

Finally, the consolidation of their psychic structure allows for greater cognitive and emotional movement between their past, present, and future. This ease of temporal movement lessens the need to disconnect and compartmentalize events and affects as necessary for a continued sense of psychological survival. This time linkage provides a sense of a personal history, of a continuity, which contributes to the calming effect on adolescents. Their increased capacity to think and deal more comfortably with their future is dependent on previous affect attunement by parents. If adolescents have internalized their world as a predictable, caring place, the continued development of self-esteem and self-regulation with the help of others, the development of a sense of competence, and self-integration through the filter of the self will proceed in a healthy and adaptive fashion. However, this is not always the case. When the sense of the world for adolescents is one of fear and unpredictability, the continued negative RIGs and FRIGs are not able to foster positive growth of self-esteem and self-esteem regulatory abilities. These adolescents are unable to soothe themselves, much like the more volatile phase of early adolescence. This continued sense of extreme vulnerability and lack of protection portends struggles or even overt psychopathology during adolescence proper or later in life.

THE EGO IDEAL: A NEW PERSPECTIVE

Returning our focus to the interactive process between adolescent and parent raises the issue of psychic conflict (Stolorow and Brandchaft, 1988) and its role in the development of the ego ideal, a concept from classical psychoanalytic theory. Within the traditional framework, the ego ideal is viewed as part of the superego that reflects what the individual wants to become, both on a conscious and unconscious level. Developmentally, the ego ideal is traditionally viewed as consolidated during adolescence proper. This consolidation fosters a renewed identification with the same-sexed parent.

The concept of the ego ideal can also be viewed as developing from the perspective of self-experiences and affect attunement. Within our theoretical framework, the continued importance of the child–parent dyad is emphasized as infants and children continue to receive messages about parental expectations, both consciously and unconsciously. Infants and children concerned with pleasing their parents and caregivers continually struggle with "moving" to the needs of their parents and caregivers in order to maintain these selfobject ties.

This need to please parents and caregivers continues in a special way in adolescence. Adolescents who have achieved some capacity for formal operational thinking begin to look increasingly to the future. As they become more involved with the future, they increasingly think about what they want to become. This is where the subtle lifelong parental expectations are taken more into consideration, depending, of course, on the nature of the ties. The most adaptive choice is made when the ambitions and goals of adolescents are facilitated by their parents, both consciously and unconsciously. These adolescents are allowed to search for their own life choices. Other pathways include adolescents who have gained a sense of self by pleasing their parents, and who consequently feel a need to follow in the pathways of parental expectations when choosing a lifestyle and career.

One example is adolescents who grow up knowing that one or both parents require them to become a physician, lawyer, teacher, or truck driver in order to make up for deficiencies of their parents' self-esteem. These adolescents know, through subtle messages from infancy onward, that their parents want them to give up their own expectations, desires, and wishes. Conversely, adolescents who have gained little from their child–parent ties may rebel from parental values and choose a very different lifestyle and career orientation. Likewise, adolescents with extremely low self-esteem may feel that certain goals and expectations are unattainable.

Some adolescents choose a lifestyle and career orientation fostered by a small group of peers (Wolf, Gedo, and Terman, 1972). These small groups can help their members formulate and later consolidate and support the achievement of their ideals. These types of groups may focus on intellectual ideas, movie stars, rock groups, or enthusiastic teachers. Whatever the focus of these groups, the group shares a common enthusiasm and deep acceptance of the various group members. In doing so, the group fosters and supports particular values and achievements, which have been labeled the ego ideal in traditional psychoanalytic thinking.

Along with the conscious and unconscious need to please or meet parental expectations, or to defy them, is the adolescents' sense of self based on self-experiences. Oftentimes adolescents lack a clear sense of self and direction in their lives because of their underlying FRIGs. These adolescents are unable to get beyond a negative self-image, which prevents them from pursuing their own talents or their uniqueness. These adolescents are more likely to get involved in drugs and counter-culture activities. They may also develop antisocial or even criminal tendencies.

When considering the superego, classical psychoanalytic writings have viewed females as having a less developed superego as well as greater difficulties with their ego ideals. This is due largely to an allegedly more difficult pathway through the oedipal phase. A number of writers, Chassequet-Smirgel (1976), Tyson (1982), and Lebe (1982, 1986) are moving away from issues of sexuality and aggression, and are instead basing their theories more on an object-relations viewpoint. These writings focus on female adolescents needing to break away from the primitive, omniscient, pregenital mother. Lang (1984) presents a comprehensive review of the struggle for females developing a sense of their femininity from a self psychological perspective. Lang's viewpoint closely follows that of the authors who, rather than viewing all female adolescents as needing to rupture the fusion with their all-powerful, pregenital mother, view the self-integration strivings of female adolescents on a continuum. While acknowledging the developmental need for self-integration, the bond between female adolescents and their mothers has to be *ruptured* only when these females have been used much of their younger lives as narcissistic extensions or selfobject ties to compensate for their mothers' narcissistic vulnerabilities and struggles. Female adolescents who have experienced their mothers and fathers as supporting their sense of self, who have fostered and encouraged self-integration, will face struggles, but not the life and death struggles so often written about in the psychoanalytic literature.

A similar dynamic is true for male adolescents. While there are numerous examples in the psychiatric literature of their need to disidentify with the pregenital mother, and the importance of the father in rescuing the son from the overpowering, pregenital mother, here too, a continuum exists. While sons have to separate from their mothers, the striving for self-integration is determined again by many factors. These factors include the intensity of the mother–son relationship, the strength of the father–son relationship, the selfobject needs of the growing child, as well as the internal perceptions and conflicts over ties with parents.

RELATIONSHIPS WITH THE FAMILY

The diminished volatility of adolescence proper makes family interactions less chaotic. There is more of a sense of give and take with parents and siblings. This change is related to the decreased egocentrism of adolescence proper and the resulting decrease in shame brought on by the consolidation of cognitive functions and decreased internal pressures and conflicts. The result is a lessened self-centeredness, a greater concern for the feelings of others, and a sense of responsibility that allows families to return to a more cohesive state. Once again, families can provide support to their teenagers who are available as selfobjects on a more mature level. Parents can now be sought out for their opinions, based on their wisdom and experience, that were earlier put down or ridiculed by their early adolescents. There is also a greater ability to discuss issues, limits, and problems maturely, rather than acting them out. In families in which the archaic grandiosity and sense of entitlement persist, dysfunctional behaviors are maintained which do not allow for maturation and autonomy.

INTERACTIONS WITH PEERS

Most adolescents tend to have very different relationships with their peers than early adolescents. For adolescents, especially those who have attained formal operational thinking, peers are more often experienced as true colleagues or true friends. With the lessened narcissistic investment, disagreements between friends lose much of the "all or nothing quality." Instead, adolescents attempt to repair misunderstandings in order to mend their friendships; this includes elements of more mature selfobject ties with their friends. Adolescents, especially those needing less archaic selfobject supports, no longer simply walk away from friends when disagreements occur. As a result, shortcomings in their friends can be accepted as part of the relationship, without the necessity of relationships being destroyed because of singular disappointments, narcissistic injuries, and the ensuing rage.

Gilligan (1982) and McDermott et al. (1984), describe alternative ways to understand the strivings for self-integration between males and females. This is particularly relevant for Gilligan, who states that Kohlberg's original work on moral development only included interviews with males. Due to this bias, only male-related issues, such as the striving for independence and being competitive, were viewed as most developmentally valued in our society. These issues are not particularly the same concerns or views of most females and some males. Instead, females tend to value relationships and cooperativeness as more important goals in life. These goals foster a greater sense of connection with family and friends. McDermott et al. (1984), along similar lines, also describes the need to "leave home," or go away to college, as the result of our society's encouraging and rewarding of this more male-oriented strive for independence.

DATING

Not all teenagers date, particularly today when adolescents tend to go out in groups. However, there is an increased comfort around members of the opposite sex. The anxiety that fostered the isolation from members of the opposite sex in early adolescence slowly gives way to a more relaxed interaction, particularly with the increased comfort of adolescents with their own body and sense of genital sexuality. When there are periods of intense anxiety with opposite sexed members, the more solid psychic foundation of adolescents allows these uncomfortable states to be more easily accepted, tolerated, and understood as only a temporary state of mind rather than an intolerable state that heralds an impending state of disorganization or self-fragmentation. This greater comfort with their own sexuality allows them to continue to develop an identification with the same-sexed parent. With encouragement and excitement from both parents, both male and female adolescents can enjoy their emerging sexuality (Tyson, 1982).

SCHOOL

School provides direction in some adolescents' search for self. For these adolescents, school helps to facilitate and consolidate a sense of competence which fosters increased self-worth and self-esteem. Successes in school can prepare these adolescents for tasks following high school, including work or college. For other adolescents, school provides a social milieu. Unfortunately, for too many adolescents, school reinforces negative self-images and a sense of failure. These adolescents are often exposed to poorly designed curriculums, poorly educated teachers who may also be uninvolved, as well as struggling with their own issues with lack of interest, a fear of boredom, and frustration.

WORK

Work can be very important to the reduction of egocentrism during adolescence. This "de-centering" (Looft, 1971) facilitates the adolescent's acquiring a perspective toward the future rather than remaining tied to the present. From a different perspective, Steinberg, Greenberger, Jacobi, and Garguque (1981) state that the work place will "facilitate the acquisition of information not taught in school, contribute to the development of responsibility and a sense of competence, lessen feelings of alienation and uselessness, and help break down inner generational barriers" (Steinberg, Greenberger, Jacobi, & Garguque, 1981, p. 142). They view the most important lesson gained from working is learning how to interact more effectively with others.

SUMMARY

Early adolescence can be seen as a crucial time in the "search for self," with adolescence proper as a time when the "search for self" is consolidated. Some of the vulnerabilities that begin in early adolescence are integrated as part of their set of organizing principles or psychic structure. In adolescence proper, as well as later in life, self-esteem and self-esteem regulation continue to be crucial aspects in the formation of organizing principles that allow for more mature ways of dealing with intense situations and affects.

Predictions about the growth and development of psychic structure can be made. The better the sense of self, the more solid the psychic foundation early adolescents and later adolescents have available to develop their future plans. Many adolescents are able to find alternative pathways to mend their primary structural defects by the development of compensatory structures (Kohut, 1971, 1977, 1984) that often focus on ideals and goals. These compensatory structures, usually developing around idealization, help to heal the various selfobject mirroring failures and misattunements. These compensatory structures are healthier than defensive structures, which only cover up, rather than repair these self-object injuries. By adolescence proper, the set of organizing principles or psychic structure should be consolidated well enough to provide an indication of how these microtraumas or more significant traumas will be compensated for or defended against.

Throughout this book, we have attempted to describe a distinctive developmental phase of life based on our understanding of self psychology and Piagetian cognitive theory. We have presented and developed several themes. First, Piagetian cognitive development, from sensorimotor thinking through formal operational thinking, is intricately intertwined with affect development and affect integration. Second, affect development is a function of the development of attunement or misattunement in the infant–parent dyad. This dyad is also quite important during early adolescence. The parental capacity to serve as a selfobject for their developing infants, children, and early adolescents, and ultimately as a facilitator, is crucial in the development of a set of organizing principles, or psychic structure. This set of organizing principles, or psychic structure, determines how adolescents perceive their capabilities to deal with the surrounding world. Third, RIGs and FRIGs are altered and reformed, and higher levels are laid down during early adolescence, which hopefully allows for a more functional and mature psychic foundation for adolescents to consolidate their "search for self."

In conclusion, as we stated in the introduction, our intent is not to be the definitive or singular theoretical viewpoint on early adolescence. We have presented a developmental theory based on affect attunement and cognitive principles which we believe has not been previously presented. The authors do hope that this book will facilitate further discussion and increased enlightenment on this unique and exciting developmental phase of life.

Bibliography

Ainsworth, M. 1974. "Infant Mother Attachment and Social Development." In *The Integration of the Child into a Social World*. Edited by M. Richars. London: Cambridge University Press.

Ausubel, D. 1950. "Negativism as a Phase of Ego Development." *American Journal of Orthopsychiatry*. Vol. 20, pp. 198–805.

Bacal, H. 1985. "Optimal Responsiveness and the Therapeutic Process." In *Progress in Self-Psychology*. Vol. 1, Edited by A. Goldberg. New York: Guilford Press, pp. 202–227.

Basch, M. 1975. "Toward a Theory that Encompasses Depression: A Revision of Existing Causal Hypotheses in Psychoanalysis." In *Depression and Human Existence*. Edited by J. Anthony and T. Benedek. Boston: Little, Brown and Co., pp. 485–534.

Basch, M. 1976. "The Concept of Affect: A Reexamination." *Journal of the American Psychoanalytic Association*. Vol. 24, No. 4, pp. 759–777.

Basch, M. 1977. "Developmental Psychology and Explanatory Theory in Psychoanalysis." In *The Annual of Psychoanalysis*, Vol. 5. New York: International Universities Press, pp. 229–263.

Basch, M. 1982. "Discussion: The Significance of Infant Developmental Studies for Psychoanalytic Theory." *Psychoanalytic Inquiry*, Vol. 1, No. 4, pp. 731–737.

Basch, M. 1983. "The Perception of Reality and the Disavowal of Meaning." In *The Annual of Psychoanalysis*, Vol. 11, pp. 125–153.

Basch, M. 1985. "Interpretation: Toward a Developmental Model." In *Kohut's Legacy*. Edited by P. Stepansky and A. Goldberg. Hillsdale, N.J.: Analytic Press, pp. 21–41.

Beebe, B. and F. Lachmann. 1988. "Mother–Infant Mutual Influence and

Precursors of Psychic Structure." In *Progress in Self Psychology,* Vol. 3, Edited by A. Goldberg. Hillsdale, N.J.: Analytic Press, pp. 33–42.

Bell, R. 1977. *Child Effects on Adults.* Hillsdale, N.J.: Halstad Press.

Benedek, T. 1959. "Parenthood as a Developmental Phase," *Journal of the American Psychoanalytic Association.* Vol. 7, pp. 389–417.

Benedek, T. 1970. "Parenthood during the Life Cycle." In *Parenthood: Its Psychology and Psychopathology.* Edited by E. Anthony and T. Benedek. Boston: Little, Brown and Co., pp. 109–136.

Berkowitz, Irving. 1983. "Emerging from Adolescence: Theoretical Discussion." In *Clinical Update in Adolescent Psychiatry.* N.J.: Nassau Publications.

Blos, P. 1967. "The Second Individuation Process of Adolescence," *The Psychoanalytic Study of the Child.* Vol. 22, pp. 162–186.

Blos, P. 1970. *The Young Child: Clinical Studies.* New York: Free Press.

Blos, P. 1979. *The Adolescent Passage: Developmental Issues.* New York: International Universities Press.

Bower, T.G.R. 1976. *A Primer of Infant Development.* San Francisco: W. H. Freeman Press.

Bowlby, J. 1958. "The Nature of the Child's Tie to His Mother." *International Journal of Psychoanalysis,* Vol. 39, pp. 350–373.

Brenner, C. 1957. "The Nature and Development of the Concept of Repression in Freud's Writings." In *The Psychoanalytic Study of the Child.* Vol. 12, pp. 19–46.

Brenner, C. 1974. "Depression, Anxiety and Affect Theory." In *International Journal of Psychoanalysis,* Vol. 55, London: Bailliere Tindall, pp. 25–32.

Brenner, C. 1980. "Metapsychology and Psychoanalytic Theory." *Psychoanalytic Quarterly.* Vol. 49, pp. 189–214.

Brody, S. 1975. "Continuity and Conflict in Maternal Behavior." Presented for panel on "Parenthood as a Development Phase." Reported by H. Parens. In *Journal of the American Psychoanalytic Association.* Vol. 23, pp. 154–165.

Burch, C. 1985. "Identity Foreclosure in Early Adolescence: A Problem of Narcissistic Equilibrium." In *Adolescent Psychiatry.* Vol. 12, pp. 145–161.

Chassequet-Smirgel, J. 1976. "Freud and Female Sexuality." *International Journal of Psychoanalysis.* Vol. 57, pp. 275–286.

Chess, S. and A. Thomas. 1963. *Behavioral Individuality in Early Childhood.* New York: New York University Press.

Cohen, R. and H. Balikov. 1974. "On the Impact of Adolescence Upon Parents," *Adolescent Psychiatry.* Vol. 3, pp. 217–236.

Cohen, R., B. Cohler, and S. Weissman. 1984. *Parenthood: A Psychodynamic Perspective.* New York: Guilford Press.

Cohen, R. and S. Weissman. 1984. "The Parenting Alliance." In *Parenthood: A Psychodynamic Perspective.* Edited by R. Cohen, B. Bertram, and S. Weissman. New York: Guilford, pp. 33–49.

Cohler, B. 1980. "Developmental Perspectives on the Psychology of the Self in Early Childhood." In *Advances of Self Psychology*. Edited by A. Goldberg. New York: International Universities Press, pp. 69–115.

Cotton, N. 1985. "The Development of Self-Esteem and Self-Esteem Regulation." In *The Development and Sustaining of Self-Esteem in Childhood*. Edited by J. Mack and S. Ablon. New York: International Universities Press, pp. 122–150.

Cowan, P. 1978. *Piaget With Feelings: Cognitive, Social, and Emotional Dimensions*. New York: Holt, Rinehart, and Winston.

Demos, V. 1982. "Affect in Early Infancy: Physiology or Psychology?" In *Psychoanalytic Inquiry.* Vol. 1, No. 4, pp. 533–574.

Demos, V. 1983. "A Perspective From Infant Research on Affect and Self-Esteem." *The Development and Sustaining of Self-Esteem in Childhood*. Edited by J. Mack, and S. Ablon. New York: International Universities Press, Inc., pp. 45–78.

Demos, V. 1984. "Empathy and Affect: Reflections on Infant Experience." In *Empathy*. Vol. II, Edited by J. Lichtenberg, M. Bornstein, and D. Silver. Hillsdale, N.J.: Analytic Press, pp. 9–34.

Demos, V. and S. Kaplan. 1986. "Motivation and Affect Reconsidered: Affect Biographies of Two Infants." In *Psychoanalysis and Contemporary Thought*. Vol. 9, pp. 147–221.

Dulit, E. 1972. "Adolescent Thinking à la Piaget: The Formal Stage." *Journal of Youth and Adolescence*. Vol. 1, No. 4, pp. 281–301.

Elkind, D. 1981. *The Hurried Child: Growing Up Too Fast, Too Soon*. Reading, Mass.: Addison–Wesley Publishing Company.

Elkind, D. 1984. *All Grown Up and No Where to Go: Teenagers in Crisis*. Reading, Mass.: Addison-Wesley Publishing Company.

Elkind, D. and R. Bowen. 1979. "Imaginary Audience Behavior in Children and Adolescents." *Developmental Psychology*. Vol. 15, No. 1, pp. 38–44.

Emde, R. 1983. "The Prerepresentational Self and Its Affective Core." *The Psychoanalytic Study of the Child*. Vol. 38, pp. 165–192.

Erikson, E. 1950. *Childhood and Society*. New York: W. W. Norton and Co.

Erikson, E. 1959. *Identity and the Life Cycle* [Psychological Monograph]. New York: International Universities Press.

Erikson, E. 1968. *Identity: Youth and Crisis*. New York: W. W. Norton and Co.

Esman, A. 1985. "A Developmental Approach to the Psychotherapy of Adolescents." *Adolescent Psychiatry*. Vol. 12, pp. 119–133.

Flavell, J. 1977. *Cognitive Development*. Englewood Cliffs, N.J.: Prentice Hall, Inc.

Freud, A. 1936. *Ego and the Mechanisms of Defense*. New York: International Universities Press.

Freud, A. 1958. "Adolescence." *Psychoanalytic Study of the Child*. Vol. 13, pp. 255–278.

Freud, A. 1965. *Normality and Pathology in Childhood*. The Writings of Anna Freud, 6. New York: International Universities Press.

Freud, S. 1905a. "Fragment of an Analysis of a Case of Hysteria." *The Standard Edition: The Complete Psychological Works of Sigmund Freud*. Edited by J. Strachey, Vol. 7. London: Hogarth Press.

Freud, S. 1905b. "Three Essays on the Theory of Sexuality." *The Standard Edition: The Complete Psychological Works of Sigmund Freud*. Edited. By J. Strachey. Vol. 7. London: Hogarth Press.

Freud, S. 1923. "The Ego and the Id." *The Standard Edition: The Complete Psychological Works of Sigmund Freud*. Edited by J. Strachey. Vol. 19. London: Hogarth Press.

GAP. 1968. *Normal Adolescence: Its Dynamics and Impact*. Vol. 6, Report #68.

Gilligan, C. 1982. *In A Different Voice: Psychological Theory and Women's Development*. Cambridge, Mass.: Harvard University Press.

Greenberg, J., and Mitchell, S. 1983. *Object Relations in Psychoanalytic Theory*. Cambridge, Mass.: Harvard University Press.

Greenspan, S. 1979. *Intelligence and Adaptation: An Integration of Psychoanalysis and Piagetian Developmental Psychology, Psychological Issues*. Vol. 12, No. 3/4, Monograph 47/48. New York: International Universities Press.

Grotstein, J. 1987. "Meaning, Meaninglessness, and the 'Black Hole': Self and Interactional Regulation as a New Paradigm for Psychoanalysis and Neuroscience, An Introduction." Unpublished manuscript.

Hall, G. S. 1904. *Adolescence: Its Psychology and Its Relations to Physiology, Anthropology, Sociology, Sex, Crime, Religion, and Education*. New York: Appleton-Century-Crafts.

Hartmann, H. 1958. *Ego Psychology and the Problem of Adaptation*. New York: International Universities Press.

Holtzman, E. 1982/83. Personal communications.

Kaufman, G. 1985. *Shame: The Power of Caring*. Cambridge, Mass.: Schenkman Books.

Kernberg, O. 1968. "The Treatment of Parents with Borderline Personality Organization." *International Journal of Psychoanalysis*. Vol. 49, No. 4, pp. 600–619.

Kernberg, O. 1982. "Self, Ego, Affects, and Drives." *Journal of the American Psychoanalytic Association*. Vol. 30, No. 4, pp. 893–917.

Kohut, H. 1971. *The Analysis of the Self: A Systematic Approach to the Psychoanalytic Treatment of Narcissistic Personality Disorders. The Psychoanalytic Study of the Child*. Monograph No. 4. New York: International Universities Press, Inc.

Kohut, H. 1972. "Thoughts on Narcissism and Narcissistic Rage." *The Psychoanalytic Study of the Child.* Vol. 27, pp. 360–400.

Kohut, H. 1977. *The Restoration of the Self.* New York: International Universities Press.

Kohut, H. 1984. *How Does Analysis Cure?.* Edited by A. Goldberg with the collaboration of P. Stepansky. Chicago: University of Chicago Press.

Kohut, H. 1987. *The Kohut Seminars on Self Psychology and Psychopathology with Adolescents and Young Adults.* Edited by M. Elson. New York: Analytic Press.

Kohut, H. and E. Wolf. 1978. "The Disorders of the Self and Their Treatment: An Outline." *International Journal of Psychoanalysis.* Vol. 59, pp. 413–425.

Krystal, H. 1981. "The Hedonic Element in Affectivity." *The Annual of Psychoanalysis.* Vol. 9, pp. 93–113.

Krystal, H. 1982. "Adolescence and the Tendencies to Develop Substance Abuse." *Psychoanalytic Inquiry.* Vol. 2, No. 4, pp. 581–617.

Krystal, H. 1982/83. "Alexithymia and the Effectiveness of Psychoanalytic Treatment." *International Journal of Psychoanalytic Psychotherapy.* Vol. 9, pp. 353–378.

Lang, J. 1984. "Notes Toward a Psychology of the Feminine Self." In *Kohut's Legacy.* Edited by P. Stepansky and A. Goldberg. Hillsdale, N.J.: Analytic Press, pp. 51–69.

Lebe, D. 1982. "Individuation of Women." *Psychoanalytic Reader.* Vol. 69, pp. 63–73.

Lebe, D. 1986. "Female Ego Ideal Conflicts in Childhood." *Journal of the American Psychoanalytic Association.* Vol. 46, pp. 22–32.

Lewis, H. 1987. "Shame and the Narcissistic Personality." In *The Many Faces of Shame.* Edited by D. Nathanson. New York: Guilford Press, pp. 93–132.

Looft, W. 1971. "Egocentrism and Social Interaction in Adolescence." *Adolescence.* Vol. 6, pp. 485–494.

Lovitz, A. 1985. "Understanding Shame in Patients with Narcissistic Conflicts." Unpublished manuscript.

Mahler, M. 1971. "A Study of the Separation–Individuation Process and its Possible Application to Borderline Phenemona in the Psychoanalytic Situation." *The Psychoanalytic Study of the Child.* Vol. 26, pp. 403–423.

Mahler, M. 1972. "On the First Three Subphases of the Separation-Individuation Process." *International Journal of Psychoanalysis.* Vol. 53, pp. 333–338.

Mahler, M., F. Pine and A. Bergman. 1975. *The Psychological Birth of the Human Infant.* New York: Basic Books.

Marohn, R. 1977. "The 'Juvenile Imposter': Some Thoughts on Narcissism and the Delinquent." In *Adolescent Psychiatry*. Vol. 5, pp. 186–92.

Marohn, R. 1979. "A Psychiatric Overview of Juvenile Delinquency." In *Adolescent Psychiatry*. Vol. 7, pp. 425–432.

Marohn, R. 1980. "Adolescent Rebellion and the Task of Separation. *Adolescent Psychiatry*. Vol. 8, pp. 173–183.

Marohn, R. 1981. "The Negative Transference in the Treatment of Juvenile Delinquents." *The Annual of Psychoanalysis*. Vol. 9, pp. 21–42.

Marohn, R., D. Offer, E. Astrov, and J. Trujillo. 1979. "Psychodynamic Types of Hospitalized Juvenile Delinquents." In *Adolescent Psychiatry*. Vol. 7, pp. 466–483.

Martin, E. 1971. "Reflections on the Early Adolescent in School." *Twelve to Sixteen: Early Adolescence*. Edited by J. Kagan and R. Coles. New York: W. W. Norton, pp. 180–196.

Masterson, J. 1968. *Treatment of the Borderline Adolescent*. New York: Brunner/Mazel.

Masterson, J. 1981. *Narcissistic and Borderline Disorders*. New York: Brunner/Mazel.

McDermott, J., A. Robillard, W. Char, J. Hsu, W. Tseng, and G. Ashton. 1984. "Reexamining the Concept of Adolescence: Differences Between Adolescent Boys and Girls in the Context of Their Families." *Annual Progress in Child Psychiatry and Development*. Vol. 15, pp. 155–165.

Miller, A. 1981. *Prisoners of Childhood: The Drama of the Gifted Child and the Search for the True Self*. New York: Basic Books.

Miller, A. 1983. *For Your Own Good: Hidden Cruelty in Child-Rearing and the Roots of Violence*. New York: Farrar, Straus, and Giroux.

Miller, A. 1984. *Thou Shalt Not Be Aware: Society's Betrayal of the Child*. New York: Farrar, Straus, and Giroux.

Miller, D. 1974. *Adolescence: Psychology, Psychotherapy, and Psychopharmacology*. New York: Jason Aronson.

Modell, A. 1981. "Does Metapsychology Still Exist?" *International Journal of Psychoanalysis*. Vol. 62, pp. 391–402.

Morrison, A. 1984. "Shame and the Psychology of the Self." In *Kohut's Legacy*. Edited by P. Stepansky and A. Goldberg. Hillsdale, N.J.: Analytic Press, pp. 71–90.

Muslin, H. 1984. "On the Resistance to Parenthood: Considerations of the Self of the Father." In *Parenthood: A Psychodynamic Perspective*. Edited by R. Cohen, B. Cohler, and S. Weissman. New York: Guilford Press, pp. 315–25.

Muuss, R. 1975. "Jean Piaget's Cognitive Theory of Adolescent Development." *Theories of Adolescence*. Third Edition, edited by R. E. Muuss. New York: Random House, pp. 178–207.

Nathanson, Donald. 1987. "A Timetable for Shame." In *Many Faces of Shame*. Edited by D. Nathanson. New York: Guilford Press, pp. 1–63.

Offer, D., E. Ostrov, and K. Howard. 1981. *The Adolescent: A Psychological Self-Portrait*. New York: Basic Books.

Offer, D. and M. Sabshin. 1984. "Adolescence: Empirical Perspectives." In *Normality and the Life Cycle*. Edited by D. Offer and M. Sabshin, pp. 76–107.

Ornstein, A. 1974. "The Dread to Repeat and the New Beginning: A Contribution to the Psychoanalysis of the Narcissistic Personality Disorders." *The Annual of Psychoanalysis*. Vol. 2, pp. 231–248.

Ornstein, A. 1981. "Self-Pathology in Childhood: Developmental and Clinical Considerations." In *Psychiatric Clinics of North America*. Vol. 4, No. 3, pp. 435–453.

Ornstein, A. 1983. "An Idealizing Transference of the Oedipal Phase." *Reflections on Self Psychology*. Edited by J. Litchtenberg and S. Kaplan, Hillsdale, N.J.: Laurence Erlbaum Associates, pp. 135–148.

Ornstein, A., C. Gropper, and J. Bogner. 1983. "Shoplifting: An Expression of Revenge and Restitution." *The Annual of Psychoanalysis*. Vol. 11, pp. 311–331.

Ornstein, A. and P. Ornstein. 1985. "Parenting as a Function of the Adult Self: A Psychoanalytic Developmental Perspective." *Parental Influences: In Health and Disease*. Edited by E. Anthony and G. Pollock. Boston/Toronto: Little, Brown and Company.

Ornstein, P. and A. Ornstein. 1980. "Formulating Interpretations in Clinical Psychoanalysis." *International Journal of Psychoanalysis*. Vol. 61, pp. 203–211.

Palombo, J. 1987. "Selfobject Transference in the Treatment of Borderline Neurocognitively Impaired Children." In *Borderline*. Vol. 1, Edited by J. Grotstein, M. Solomon, and J. Lang. Hillsdale, N.J.: Analytic Press, pp. 317–345.

Papoušek, H. and M. Papoušek. 1983. "Interactional Failures: Their Origins and Significance in Infant Psychiatry." In *Frontiers of Infant Psychiatry*. Edited by J. Call, E. Galenson, and R. Tyson, New York: Basic Books, pp. 31–37.

Paul, N. 1970. "Parental Empathy." In *Parenthood: Its Psychology and Psychopathology*. Edited by J. Anthony and T. Benedek. Boston: Little Brown and Co., pp. 337–352.

Peterfreund, E. 1975a. "How Does the Analyst Listen? On Models and Strategies in the Psychoanalytic Process," *Psychoanalysis and Contemporary Science*, Vol. 4, pp. 59–101.

Peterfreund, E. 1975b. "The Need for a New General Theoretical Frame of Reference for Psychoanalysis." In *Psychoanalytic Quarterly*. Vol. 44, no. 4, pp. 534–549.

Peterfreund, E. 1983. *Process of Psychoanalytic Theory: Models & Strategies.* Hillsdale, N.J.: Analytic Press.

Piaget, J. 1950. *The Psychology of Intelligence.* London: Routledge.

Piaget, J. 1972. "The Relation of Affectivity to Intelligence in the Mental Development of the Child." In *Childhood Psychopathology: An Anthology of Basic Readings.* Edited by S. Harrison and J. McDermott. New York: International Universities Press, pp. 167–175.

Piaget, J. 1975. "Intellectual Development of the Adolescent." *The Psychology of Adolescence: Essential Readings.* Edited by A. Esman. New York: International Universities Press, pp. 104–108.

Pine, Fred. 1985. *Developmental Theory and Clinical Processes.* New Haven: Yale University Press.

Pulaski, M. 1971. *Understanding Piaget: An Introduction to Children's Cognitive Development.* New York: Harper and Row.

Richmond, M. and M. Sklansky. 1984. "Structural Change in Adolescence." *Late Adolescence.* Edited by D. Brockman. New York: International Universities Press, pp. 97–121.

Rinsley, D. 1978. "Borderline Psychopathology: A Review of Actiology, Dynamics and Treatment." *International Review of Psychoanalysis.* Vol. 5, pp. 45–54.

Rinsley, D. 1980. *Treatment of the Severely Disturbed Adolescent.* New York: Jason Aronson.

Robertson, J. and J. Robertson. 1971. "Young Children in Brief Separation: A Fresh Look." *Psychoanalytic Study of the Child.* Vol. 26, pp. 264–315.

Rosenberg, 1979. *Conceiving the Self.* New York: Basic Books.

Sarnoff, C. 1987. *Psychotherapeutic Strategies in Late Latency through Early Adolescence.* Northvale, N.J.: Jason Aronson Inc.

Schafer, R. 1968. *Aspects of Internalization.* New York: International Universities Press.

Schafer, R. 1979. "Character, Ego-Syntonicity, and Character Change." *Journal of the American Psychoanalytic Association.* Vol. 27, No. 4, pp. 867–891.

Schave, D. 1981. "The Center of the Universe: Formal Operational Thinking in Early Adolescence." Twelfth Annual Piagetian Conference, University of Southern California. Los Angeles, California.

Schave, D. 1985. "The Center of the Universe: Early Adolescence." Presentation, Western Regional Conference, American Society for Adolescent Psychiatry, Scottsdale, Arizona.

Schimel, J. 1974. "Two Alliances in the Treatment of Adolescents: Toward a Working Alliance with Parents and a Therapeutic Alliance with the Adolescent." *Journal of the American Academy of Psychoanalysis.* Vol. 2, No. 3, pp. 243–253.

Schneider, C. 1987. "A Mature Sense of Shame." In *Many Faces of Shame*. Edited by D. Nathanson. New York: Guilford Press, pp. 194–213.

Schwaber, E. 1983. "Perspective on Psychoanalytic Listening." *The Psychoanalytic Study of the Child*. Vol. 38, pp. 519–546.

Socarides, D. and R. Stolorow. 1984/85. "Affects and Selfobjects." *The Annual of Psychoanalysis*. Vol. 12/13, pp. 105–119.

Spitz, R. 1945. "Hospitalization: An Inquiry Into the Genesis of Psychiatric Conditions in Early Childhood." *The Psychoanalytic Study of the Child*. Vol. 1, pp. 53–74.

Stechler, G. and S. Kaplan. 1980. "The Development of the Self." *The Psychoanalytic Study of the Child*. Vol. 35, pp. 85–105.

Steinberg, L., E. Greenberger, E. Jacobi, and L. Garguque. 1981. "Early Work Experience: A Partial Antidote for Adolescent Egocentrism." *Journal of Youth and Adolescence*. Vol. 10, No. 2, pp. 141–157.

Stern, D. 1985. *The Interpersonal World of the Infant: A View from Psychoanalysis and Developmental Psychology*. New York: Basic Books.

Stoller, R. 1968. *Sex and Gender: On the Development of Masculinity and Femininity*. New York: Science House.

Stolorow, R. 1987. "Affects and Selfobjects." In Stolorow, R., B. Brandchaft. and G. Atwood. *Psychoanalytic Treatment: An Intersubjective Approach*. Hillsdale, N.J.: Analytic Press.

Stolorow, R. and G. Atwood. 1987. "From the Subjectivity of Science to the Science of Subjectivity." In *Theories of the Unconscious and Theories of the Self*. Edited by R. Stern. Hillsdale, N.J.: Analytic Press.

Stolorow, R. and B. Brandchaft. 1988. "Developmental Failure and Psychic Conflict." In *Psychoanalytic Psychology*. Vol. 3, No. 4, pp. 241–253.

Sugarman, A. and C. Kurash. 1982. "Marijuana Abuse, Transitional Experience, and the Borderline Adolescent." In *Psychoanalytic Inquiry*. Vol. 2, No. 4, pp. 519–538.

Tolpin, M. 1974. "The Daedalus Experience: A Developmental Vicissitude of the Grandiose Fantasy." *The Annual of Psychoanalysis*. Vol. 2, pp. 213–228.

Tolpin, M. 1978. "Self-Objects and Oedipal Objects: A Crucial Developmental Distinction." *The Psychoanalytic Study of the Child*. Vol. 33, pp. 167–184.

Tolpin, M. 1980. "Discussion of 'Psychoanalytic Developmental Theories of the Self: An Integration.' By Morton Shane and Estelle Shane." In *Advances in Self Psychology*. Edited by A. Goldberg. New York: International Universities Press, pp. 47–68.

Tolpin, M. 1983. "Corrective Emotional Experience: A Self-Psychological Reevaluation." *The Future of Psychoanalysis*. Edited by A. Goldberg. New York: International Universities Press, pp. 363–379.

Tolpin, M. 1987. "Injured Self-Cohesion: Developmental, Clinical, and Theoretical Perspectives." In *The Borderline Patient: Emerging Concepts in Diagnosis, Psychodynamics, and Treatment*. Vol. 1, Edited by J. Grotstein, M. Solomon, and J. Lang. Hillsdale, N.J.: Analytic Press, pp. 233–249.

Tolpin, M. and H. Kohut. 1980. "The Disorders of the Self: The Psychopathology of the First Years of Life." In *The Course of Life: Psychoanalytic Contributions toward Understanding Personality Development*. Vol. 1, *Infancy and Early Childhood*. Edited by S. Greenspan and G. Pollock. Adelphi, Md.: NIMH, pp. 425–442.

Tomkins, S. 1980. "Affect as Amplification: Some Modifications in Theory." In *Emotion: Theory, Research, and Experience*. Edited by R. Plutchick and H. Kellerman. New York: Academic Press, pp. 141–164.

Tomkins, S. 1987. "Shame." In *The Many Faces of Shame*. Edited by D. Nathanson. New York: Guilford Press, pp. 133–161.

Tyson, P. 1982. "A Developmental Line of Gender Identity, Gender Role, and Choice of Love Object." In *Journal of the American Psychoanalytic Association*. Vol. 30, pp. 61–86.

Wilson, A. 1987. Personal communication.

Winnicott, D. W. 1945. "Primitive Emotional Development." In *Collected Papers*. New York: Basic Books, 1958, pp. 145–156.

Winnicott, D. W. 1951. "Transitional Objects and Transitional Phenomena." In *Collected Papers*. New York: Basic Books, 1958, pp. 229–242.

Winnicott, D. 1953. "Transitional Objects and Transitional Phenomena." *International Journal of Psychoanalysis*. Vol. 34, pp. 89–97.

Winnicott, D. 1958. "The Capacity to be Alone." *International Journal of Psychoanalysis*. Vol. 39, pp. 416–420.

Winnicott, D. 1960. "The Theory of the Parent–Infant Relationship." *International Journal of Psychoanalysis*. Vol. 41, pp. 585–595.

Winnicott, D. 1965. "Ego Distortion in Terms of True and False Self." In *Maturational Processes and the Facilitating Environment*. New York: International Universities Press.

Winnicott, D. 1970. "The Mother-Infant Experience of Mutuality." In *Parenthood: Its Psychology and Psychopathology*. Edited by E. Anthony and T. Benedek. Boston: Little, Brown and Co., pp. 245–256.

Wolf, E. 1980. "On the Developmental Line of Selfobject Relations." In *Advances in Self Psychology*. Edited by A. Goldberg. New York: International Universities Press, pp. 117–130.

Wolf, E., J. Gedo, and D. Terman. 1972. "On the Adolescent Process as a Transformation of the Self." *Journal of Youth and Adolescence*. Vol. 1, No. 3, pp. 257–272.

Woodward, M. 1965. "Piaget's Theory." In *Modern Perspectives in Child*

Psychiatry. Edited by J. Howell. Springfield, Ill.: Charles Thomas, pp. 58–84.

Wurmser, L. 1981. *The Mask of Shame*. Baltimore: Johns Hopkins University Press.

Index

ABOUT THE AUTHORS

DOUGLAS SCHAVE, M.D., is a member and has been Division Chief of the Department of Family and Child Psychiatry at the Cedar-Sinai Medical Center in Los Angeles, and is also in private practice with Barbara Schave. He is Past President of the Southern California Society for Adolescent Psychiatry and is currently a Candidate at the Southern California Psychoanalytic Institute.

BARBARA SCHAVE, Ed.D., Ph.D., is in a private practice in clinical psychology with Douglas Schave. She is the author of *Identity and Intimacy in Twins* and is the coauthor of two textbooks on education.